Confirmation

The Baby in Solomon's Court

by
Paul Turner

Paulist Press ◊ *New York* ◊ *Mahwah, N.J.*

The publisher gratefully acknowledges use of the following: "The Baptismal Covenant I" copyright © 1976, 1980, 1985, 1989 The United Methodist Publishing House. Excerpted from *The United Methodist Hymnal* by permission. "The Baptismal Covenant III" copyright © 1964, 1965, 1966 The United Methodist Publishing House. Excerpted from *The United Methodist Hymnal* by permission. Excerpts from "Holy Baptism" and "Affirmation of Baptism" reprinted from *Lutheran Book of Worship*, copyright © 1978, by permission of Augsburg Fortress. Excerpts from *The Book of Common Prayer* published by The Church Hymnal Corporation. Excerpts from "Age of Confirmation: Sacred Congregation on Sacraments, June 30, 1932" and "Instruction for a Simple Priest Administering the Sacrament of Confirmation: Sacred Congregation on Sacraments, May 20, 1934" © *Canon Law Digest*. Excerpts from *Code of Canon Law* © 1983, Canon Law Society of America. All rights reserved. Excerpts from *Lutheran Worship* © 1982, Concordia Publishing House. All rights reserved. Excerpts from the English translation of *Rite of Baptism for Children* 1969, International Committee on English in the Liturgy, Inc. (ICEL); excerpts from the English translation of *Rite of Confirmation*, Second Edition 1975, ICEL; excerpts from the English translation of *Rite of Christian Initiation of Adults* 1985, ICEL. All rights reserved. Excerpts from *Holy Baptism and Services for the Renewal of Baptism* (Supplemental Liturgical Resource 2). Copyright © 1985 The Westminster Press. Used by permission of Westminster/John Knox Press. Translated excerpts from "The Theology of the Liturgy: The Three Sacraments of Christian Initiation" by Archbishop Joseph Tawil reprinted with permission.

Copyright © 1993 by
Paul Turner

Turner, Paul, 1953–
    Confirmation: the baby in Solomon's court/by Paul Turner.
      p. cm.
    Includes bibliographical references and index.
    ISBN 0-8091-3370-9
    1. Confirmation—Catholic Church.   2. Catholic Church—Liturgy.
    3. Confirmation—Comparative studies.   I. Title.
    BX2210.T87 1993
    265'.2—dc20   92-32094
                                                        CIP

Published by Paulist Press
997 Macarthur Boulevard
Mahwah, New Jersey 07430

Printed and bound in the
United States of America

Contents

ALEXIAE VILLELMOQUE TURNER, QUI
ARBITRIS RELICTIS
APPROBATIONIBUS NUNQUAM EXQUISITIS
AUCTOREM DOCUIT
AUSCULTARE UTRIMQUE
ANTE RES QUAM IUDICARET
ATQUE CIRCUMSPICERE IN UTRAMQUE PARTEM
ANTE VIAM QUAM TRANSIRET
AMANTER EXPLICATIO HAEC DEDICATUR

ACKNOWLEDGMENTS

I wish to thank

St. Regis Parish, which supported
The librarians, who hunted
The ministers, who sympathized
Ronnie Scott & Joe Egender, who advised
Thom Morris, who conceived
Hippolytus, who recorded
(Pseudo-?) Faustus of Riez, who confused
and God, the source of wisdom.

P.T.

Introduction

"Is that grease?"

The six year old's stage whisper caught me off guard. It was not the ritual question I expected to hear in the middle of the Easter Vigil. The youngest candidate for confirmation that year still dripped from the waters of baptism.

Six is young for confirmation, but since Allen's big brother was being baptized at the same liturgy, and since his catechists believed he fit anyone's description of "catechetical age,"[1] we agreed he was ready for baptism, confirmation, and eucharist. Allen questioned me after I had already anointed six adults and had worked my way to him, my hand aromatic with chrism. His question proved beyond any doubt that he had hit catechetical age.

I had fielded many a question about confirmation—from professors, bishops, directors of confirmation programs, parents, teens, catechumens, candidates, relatives, and unsuspecting innocent bystanders who got much more information than they ever wanted to know. (Allen stood perilously near this group.) People want to know a lot about confirmation: What's the appropriate age? Is it a sacrament of initiation or of commitment? If I was confirmed as a Lutheran, why do I have to be confirmed as a Catholic? Why does our parish require a two year preparation for teens to be confirmed? And so on.

But of all the questions I'd heard, this one—whispered unawares into my portable microphone at the Easter Vigil—was new.

"Is that grease?"

1

"Well, yes, sort of." It is best to be honest with six year olds.
"Oh, gross!"

The response came not from Allen but from the college co-ed next in line. I could have gone on with my explanation—that chrism is far superior to grease since it is made from oil and perfume and that it can be consecrated only by a bishop and that it is used only rarely in the church. . . . But this was liturgy, not catechesis. And besides, Allen had already nodded. His question was anatomical, not theological. So I smeared the forehead of his grinning face and shot an anticipatory glance to the young lady behind him, as if to say, "You're next." She trembled at her confirmation.

Some questions about confirmation can be answered peaceably; others produce shock. Confirmation is currently being celebrated for many different occasions, according to different models. Confusion exists because these models fight each other against cohesion. Confusion also exists because any single model of confirmation contains ambiguities and inconsistencies. Questions about this sacrament can be well answered after gaining some familiarity with its many forms.

This book will present seven different models of confirma-. tion. They derive from the liturgical books and pastoral practice of several churches. I write from the perspective of an American Roman Catholic. These models will be found in other countries—Americans are not alone in our experience of multiple forms of confirmation. And other churches have models of confirmation which could be added. I have limited my scope to control the material for this book. I hope my choices will not offend, but open discussion for the perspectives of other churches and nations.

The seven models are as follows:

1) Christian Initiation of Adults. Confirmation immediately follows the baptism of adult catechumens.

2) Chrismation. The Eastern Rites chrismate (confirm) all new members, including infants, immediately after baptism.

3) Protestant-Anglican Churches. Many churches of the Reform and the Anglicans offer confirmation to their members.

4) Catholic Initiation. Catholics confirm new members who were previously baptized in another church.

5) Confirmation of Children. Children baptized as infants celebrate confirmation at a later age.

6) Adolescent Confirmation. A growing movement around the world suggests that teenage years are more appropriate than childhood years for the confirmation of those baptized as infants.

7) Persons in Danger of Death. An abbreviated rite of confirmation is provided for the dying who were never confirmed throughout their life.

In each of the chapters that follow I will explore one of these models. Each chapter will explain why this model developed and how it interprets the meaning of confirmation. I then critique its practice. It seems to me that each model influences the others, and this leakage causes inconsistencies within each form and for confirmation as a whole.

The purpose of this book is to explain the complexities of the word "confirmation" by exploring the different forms of its celebration. In doing so, I hope to equip the reader to join in the critique and the conversation.

Confirmation marks a glorious moment in the life of a Christian: the giving of the Holy Spirit. But the confusion surrounding the sacrament has created a situation that demands a decision worthy of Solomon. I pray for an ecclesial gift of wisdom.

Paul Turner
Before the Chrism Mass
9 April 1992

1
Christian Initiation of Adults

Introduction

Confirmation accompanies baptism for unbaptized people who join the Catholic Church. Adults and young children alike enter a period of formation called the catechumenate. When they complete this period, they celebrate three sacraments in the same ceremony: baptism, confirmation, and eucharist, the "sacraments of initiation." In 1972 the Catholic Church published the order of Christian initiation of adults to fully explain the rites and processes of preparation.[2]

This chapter will explain what confirmation means, how it is celebrated, and the meaning of its ritual symbols. Some concerns conclude the chapter.

What Confirmation Means

Confirmation helps express the church's teaching on salvation. It also celebrates the activity of the Holy Spirit in individual members, stimulating them to bear witness to the faith and foster the growth of the church.

The Teaching on Salvation

All sacraments are symbols; these ritual signs make something else present. Confirmation symbolizes the Holy Spirit's mission in the world, and the Christian's participation in that mission.

What's important in this model of adult initiation is not just the ritual of confirmation, but its placement right after baptism. Here, confirmation expresses God's complete plan for redemption. According to the order of Christian initiation of adults,

> The conjunction of the two celebrations signifies the unity of the paschal mystery, the close link between the mission of the Son and the outpouring of the Holy Spirit, and the connection between the two sacraments through which the Son and the Holy Spirit come with the Father to those who are baptized.[3]

Placing confirmation immediately after baptism thus joins the gift of the Spirit to the mission of Jesus. This text best explains the meaning of confirmation in adult initiation.

Confirmation is initiation here. Sharing the baptismal ceremony, confirmation celebrates the gift of the Holy Spirit now at work in the new Christian. Confirmation highlights one dimension of initiation: the outpouring of the Holy Spirit. The confirmation of new Christians depends so much on baptism that the two are celebrated together.

This dependence holds so strong that even under exceptional circumstances when the ritual of initiation must be abbreviated, confirmation still follows baptism, even though other parts of the ceremony are omitted.[4] For example, sickness, travel, change of residence, or the nearness of death may cause the period of the catechumenate to be reduced, or the ritual of initiation itself to be shortened. But when this happens, the priest or bishop who baptizes does not omit confirmation, since it expresses the fullness of God's plan.

The code of canon law supports the church's belief about salvation. This belief finds expression not only in the liturgy (in celebrating baptism and confirmation together), but also in the directives of church law. The universal laws of the Catholic Church were first codified in 1917;[5] they were revised in 1983 under the title, *Code of Canon Law*.[6] There one finds the following:

> The sacraments of baptism, confirmation, and the Most Holy Eucharist are so interrelated that they are required for full Christian initiation.[7]

The National Conference of Catholic Bishops (NCCB) repeats this same point. The NCCB is one of many conferences of bishops throughout the world. These canonical bodies deliberate concerns for the church in the geographical area they oversee. In 1986 the NCCB approved National Statutes for the Catechumenate,[8] including the following:

> In order to signify clearly the interrelation or coalescence of the three sacraments which are required for full Christian initiation (canon 842/2), adult candidates, including children of catechetical age, are to receive baptism, confirmation, and eucharist in a single eucharistic celebration.[9]

"Children of catechetical age" are those capable of catechesis, those who can learn about the church and model their lives after Christ. This age is sometimes called "age of reason" or "age of discretion."[10] The order of Christian initiation of adults treats such children as adults: If unbaptized, they are eligible for confirmation at the time of their baptism.

By receiving all three sacraments, newly initiated Christians become symbols of God's action in the world. That is why canon law advises that confirmation immediately follow the baptism of adults:

> Unless a grave reason prevents it, an adult who is baptized is to be confirmed immediately after baptism and participate in the celebration of the Eucharist, also receiving Communion.[11]

In adult initiation, confirmation expresses the role of the Holy Spirit in God's plan of salvation. This plan is realized in the life of individuals who, through baptism, experience new life in Christ and membership in his body for the first time.

The Holy Spirit in Individuals

Confirmation accomplishes two goals for individuals: It confers the gift of the Holy Spirit, and it anoints Christians to become more like Christ.

The two goals of confirmation can be seen in its two primary symbols, the prayer for the seven gifts of the Holy Spirit and the anointing with chrism. The General Introduction to the order of Christian initiation of adults makes the same point:

> By signing us with the gift of the Spirit, confirmation makes us more completely the image of the Lord and fills us with the Holy Spirit.[12]

The first goal, the outpouring of the Holy Spirit, surfaces in the prayer over those to be confirmed:

> Send your Holy Spirit upon them
> to be their helper and guide.
> Give them the spirit of wisdom and understanding,
> the spirit of right judgment and courage,
> the spirit of knowledge and reverence.
> Fill them with the spirit of wonder and awe in your presence.[13]

When the priest or bishop who confirms introduces this prayer, he invites the people to pray that the Holy Spirit will "strengthen" the newly baptized "with his gifts."[14]

The "gift" of the Spirit is manifested in "gifts." Traditionally, the church enumerates the seven gifts of this prayer ("the spirit of . . .") as evidence of the primary gift of the Holy Spirit.

The seven gifts are inspired by a text from Isaiah. There the prophet describes the qualities of Israel's new ruler, coming from Jesse's dynasty:

> A shoot shall sprout from the stump of Jesse,
> and from his roots a bud shall blossom.
> The spirit of the Lord shall rest upon him:
> a spirit of wisdom and of understanding,
> A spirit of counsel and of strength,
> a spirit of knowledge and of fear of the Lord,
> and his delight shall be the fear of the Lord.[15]

By quoting this text, the prayer of confirmation implies that the royal prophecy has two additional dimensions: It foreshadows the coming of Christ—who would perfectly fulfill the qualities of the expected ruler—and it alludes to the activity of the Holy Spirit in salvation. In addition, the prayer personalizes the text by its liturgical usage: It asks that the Spirit which filled Christ will now fill those to be confirmed. So the prayer masterfully weaves the role of the Holy Spirit in universal salvation with the

Holy Spirit in salvation. In addition, the prayer personalizes the text by its liturgical usage: It asks that the Spirit which filled Christ will now fill those to be confirmed. So the prayer masterfully weaves the role of the Holy Spirit in universal salvation with the Spirit's role in the individual Christian life. Further, while the prayer addresses the first goal of the individual's confirmation, the gift of the Spirit, it implies the second goal, becoming more like Christ.

This second goal is made clear in the anointing with chrism. The history of chrism reaches back to the ancient Hebrew custom of anointing priests, prophets, and kings. Chrism is a perfumed oil used in the church today for infant baptism, confirmation, priesthood ordination, and the consecration of the altar in a church. Only a bishop may consecrate this oil, in a special Mass celebrated each year near the end of lent.[16] Through his prayer, the Holy Spirit enlivens this oil for its holy use.

The bishop may offer one of two prayers. The first option prays for the Holy Spirit to come to the oil:

> And so, Father, we ask you to bless ✚ this oil you have
>   created.
> Fill it with the power of your Holy Spirit
> through Christ your Son.
> It is from him that chrism takes its name
> and with chrism you have anointed
> for yourself priests and kings,
> prophets and martyrs.
>
> Make this chrism a sign of life and salvation
> for those who are to be born again in the waters of baptism.
> Wash away the evil they have inherited from sinful Adam,
> and when they are anointed with this holy oil
> make them temples of your glory,
> radiant with the goodness of life
> that has its source in you.
>
> Through this sign of chrism
> grant them royal, priestly, and prophetic honor,
> and clothe them with incorruption.
> Let this be indeed the chrism of salvation

for those who will be born again of water and the Holy Spirit.
May they come to share eternal life
in the glory of your kingdom.[17]

The second option prays for the coming of the Spirit on those
to be anointed:

And so, Father, by the power of your love,
make this mixture of oil and perfume
a sign and source ✚ of your blessing.
Pour out the gifts of your Holy Spirit
on our brothers and sisters who will be anointed with it.
Let the splendor of holiness shine on the world
from every place and thing
signed with this oil.

Above all, Father, we pray
that through this sign of your anointing
you will grant increase to your Church
until it reaches the eternal glory
where you, Father, will be the all in all,
together with Christ your Son,
in the unity of the Holy Spirit,
for ever and ever.[18]

This second prayer defines chrism as a mixture of oil and
perfume. Traditionally, the bishop mixes olive oil with balsam.
Balsam is a gum from a tree called the *lentiscus*; an old legend
maintains that *lentiscus* was also the genus of wood for the cross
of Christ.[19] Today the bishop may resort to other oils and
perfumes.[20]

Consecrated by the bishop, chrism becomes a symbol of the
bishop's ministry. A priest who confirms still makes present the
bishop's work when he anoints with chrism.

Chrism symbolizes Christ and the Holy Spirit. The word
"Christ," meaning "Anointed One," shares the same origins as
the word "chrism." Anointing with chrism, then, symbolizes a
sharing in the role of Jesus Christ as priest, prophet, and king.
However, since this oil has been consecrated by the presence of
the Holy Spirit, it also symbolizes the gift of the Spirit on those

confirmed. For this reason, the priest or bishop says these words as he anoints those to be confirmed: "Be sealed with the Gift of the Holy Spirit."[21]

The texts which comment on confirmation frequently use terms of degree to describe what this sacrament does. The General Introduction of the order of Christian initiation of adults quoted above says confirmation makes one "more completely" the image of the Lord.[22] The invitation for the people to pray looks for the Holy Spirit to "strengthen" those to be confirmed.[23]

These terms function more to distinguish confirmation from baptism than to admonish a spiritual growth which requires time. Baptism, like confirmation, confers the Holy Spirit, but in addition it incorporates one into the body of Christ, forgives sin, and begins the Christian life. In adult initiation, confirmation follows immediately upon baptism. It provides no time for spiritual growth. "Strengthening" refers to God's gift of the Spirit, not to the individual's moral development. It means that the gift of the Spirit in confirmation acknowledges the gift of the Spirit in baptism. The point of these terms is to honor baptism, not to imply that those who aspire to confirmation should now prove their worthiness.

Thus, terms of degree do not refer to a spiritual growth that happens over a period of time; they refer to a deepening of the effects of baptism through a continuation of the same ritual of initiation. In other words, confirmation in the model of adult initiation does not celebrate that one has become "more completely" like Christ through a more faithful living of the Gospel; rather, it celebrates the continuing ritual of initiation begun with baptism, soon to reach its perfection in eucharist, but now experiencing a "strengthening" or a "sealing" through the symbols of confirmation.

What does confirmation mean for individuals? It strengthens them with the gift of the Holy Spirit and anoints them to become more like Christ.

What Confirmation Accomplishes

The church expects that confirmation will have an effect on the lives of those who receive it. Namely, it expects them to bear witness to Christ before all the world. The result of that testimony will be the growth of the Christian community.

The General Introduction of the order of Christian initiation of adults says people are confirmed

> so that (they) may bear witness . . . before all the world and work to bring the Body of Christ to its fullness as soon as possible.[24]

Confirmation, then, is more than a symbol of God's plan, and more than a gift of the Holy Spirit. It is a motivational force for proclaiming the Gospel in the world.

How Confirmation Is Celebrated

Confirming adults at the time of their baptism causes certain peculiarities in the way the sacrament is celebrated: the age of those to be confirmed, the catechesis they receive, the time of year for the ceremony, and the minister who leads it.

The Age of Those To Be Confirmed

At what age should people be confirmed according to this model? The answer is simple: At whatever age they are baptized.

In a passage that surely inspired canon 866 quoted above, the order of Christian initiation of adults says,

> adults are not to be baptized without receiving confirmation immediately afterward, unless some serious reason stands in the way.[25]

So "age" does not really matter here. Occasion matters. The occasion of baptism makes it time for confirmation.

Does the same hold true for unbaptized children? Yes, if they have reached catechetical age. According to canon law, the laws of the church regarding baptism of adults are the same for these children of catechetical age:

What is prescribed in the canons on the baptism of an adult is applicable to all who are no longer infants but have attained the use of reason.[26]

These children become catechumens to prepare for baptism. Then, they

will receive the sacrament of baptism, the bishop or priest who baptizes them will also confer confirmation, and the children will for the first time participate in the liturgy of the eucharist.[27]

The same is recorded in the National Statutes of the NCCB:

Since children who have reached the use of reason are considered, for purposes of Christian initiation, to be adults (canon 852/1) . . . they should receive the sacraments of baptism, confirmation, and eucharist at the Easter Vigil, together with the older catechumens.[28]

The reason children receive confirmation at baptism is the same reason adults do: The rites of initiation together symbolize God's plan of salvation.[29] These sacraments are not to be separated except for grave circumstances.

Canon law is quite strong on this point. It says priests are permitted to confirm "one who is no longer an infant,"[30] and the priest "who has this faculty must use it for those in whose favor the faculty was granted."[31] That means that children who have completed a period of preparation—a catechumenate—and are baptized, have a right to confirmation, and the priest who baptizes must confirm them immediately.

This will seem unusual to many people. And it is, simply because of numbers: The number of catechized children baptized into the church is smaller than the number of infants. Those countless infants are confirmed later in life, and that is why many people assume that delayed confirmation is normal. But the main reason confirmation is delayed for them is because the infants were not at catechetical age when they were baptized. If the confirmation of young children seems unusual, it's because it is infrequent. However, the practice fully adheres to the purpose of confirmation as a rite of adult initiation.

Some might be tempted then to delay the baptism of all infants until they reach catechetical age when confirmation may be administered immediately. But the order of baptism for children says, "An infant should be baptized within the first weeks after birth."[32] Canon law concurs: "Parents are obliged to see to it that infants are baptized within the first weeks after birth."[33] Thus the church preserves a sense that children born of Christian households have a right to this first sacrament, even before the use of reason.[34]

Some parishes baptizing children of catechetical age might be tempted to delay their confirmation. In this way, these children could approach confirmation like those baptized as infants: They could prepare the same way, and they could be confirmed together. But the National Statutes of the NCCB cautioned about this:

> Some elements of the ordinary catechetical instruction of baptized children before their reception of the sacraments of confirmation and eucharist may be appropriately shared with catechumens of catechetical age. Their condition and status as catechumens, however, should not be compromised or confused, nor should they receive the sacraments of initiation in any sequence other than that determined in the ritual of Christian initiation.[35]

So some instruction may be taken together, but confirmation should not be displaced after first eucharist.

Does that mean they could be confirmed at a date later than baptism as long as they do not receive communion till then? No. As stated above, only for grave reasons is confirmation separated from baptism for these children.[36] That means something like danger of death, not convenience in catechesis.

The age of confirmation, then—for this model—is the age of baptism. What is the age of baptism? The age when preparatory catechetical formation is complete.

Appropriate Catechesis

In the model of adult initiation, catechesis for confirmation is the same as catechesis for baptism. Both sacraments are administered together and form part of the same rites of initiation.

The order of Christian initiation of adults describes different stages for the candidates for initiation. Each stage establishes its own goals for catechesis. These goals pertain to confirmation as well as to baptism and eucharist.

♦ For example, to become catechumens, people must show "evidence of the first faith, . . . of an initial conversion and intention to change their lives and to enter into a relationship with God in Christ."[37] Catechesis, then, is directed toward repentance, prayer, and community.

♦ During the catechumenate itself, catechesis is to be "gradual and complete in its coverage, accommodated to the liturgical year, and solidly supported by celebrations of the word."[38] Thus, while catechumens are growing in the Christian way of life, catechesis should include the teachings of the church and a sense of the mystery of salvation. All instruction is rooted in the Scriptures heard on Sundays and feasts of the year.

♦ Before beginning their final weeks of preparation, "catechumens are expected to have undergone a conversion in mind and in action and to have developed a sufficient acquaintance with Christian teaching as well as a spirit of faith and charity."[39] This allows them to make their final preparations for initiation during a time of spiritual recollection and interior reflection.[40] Catechesis has a more spiritual goal at this stage.

♦ After their initiation, they spend time together "to grow in deepening their grasp of the paschal mystery and in making it part of their lives."[41] This they accomplish by meditating on the Gospel, sharing the eucharist, and doing charity. Catechesis has moved from the catechetical group to the world.

The confirmation of catechumens requires the same preparation as baptism. To prepare for confirmation is to prepare for a complete change of life. Catechesis involves more than learning the teachings of the church—it means living a moral life according to the Gospel and taking an ever greater role in the Christian community.

With regard to children eligible for confirmation under this model, the nature of catechesis differs from that for adults. Children are still developing moral responsibility and the ability to grasp ideas.

The order of Christian initiation of adults notes their special condition:

Such children are capable of receiving and nurturing a personal faith and of recognizing an obligation in conscience. But they cannot yet be treated as adults because, at this stage of their lives, they are dependent on their parents or guardians and are still strongly influenced by their companions and their social surroundings.[42]

Consequently, the order adapts its expectations of their progress and the nature of their catechesis:

The Christian initiation of these children requires both a conversion that is personal and somewhat developed, in proportion to their age, and the assistance of the education they need.[43]

Even among children, catechesis still involves conversion of heart, moral development, and knowledge about the church—but "in proportion to their age."

When To Celebrate Confirmation

The proper time to celebrate confirmation in this model should be clear: at the time of baptism. And according to the order of Christian initiation of adults that should be at the Easter Vigil,[44] when catechetical formation has been completed. This imitates the practice in the early history of the church, and emphasizes the paschal mystery celebrated in these sacraments: Jesus has risen from the dead, and he shares his new life with the church, notably in its new members.

The Minister

The ordinary minister of confirmation is the same as for baptism: the bishop. But under certain circumstances a priest may administer both sacraments.

The order of confirmation calls the bishop the "original" minister.[45] So does Vatican II.[46] But the code of canon law calls him the "ordinary" minister.[47] The canonical term might disappoint those who recognize that the priest is the ordinary minister of confirmation in the Eastern Rites,[48] or those who prefer the inherent freedom of a term like "original," which binds the bishop historically and theologically to the ministry of confirmation, but not practically. The term "original" seems to imply a broader participation in the ministry of confirmation. However, the canonical term does not contradict the implications of the liturgical one. The code of canon law pertains to the Roman Catholic Church, the Latin Rite. So the canonical term "ordinary minister" simply acknowledges the long-standing Roman custom: the bishop ordinarily administers confirmation.[49]

The role of the bishop is made clear by the National Statutes of the NCCB:

> The diocesan bishop is the proper minister of the sacraments of initiation for adults, including children of catechetical age.[50]

However, most dioceses have too many candidates each year for the bishop alone to initiate. So he shares this ministry with priests. As mentioned above, a priest who baptizes anyone "who is no longer an infant" has permission to confirm,[51] and the order of Christian initiation of adults says the same.[52] Further, the priest must confirm those for whom he has permission.[53] In sharing the ministry, the bishop still remains a part of confirmation through the priest's use of chrism which the bishop consecrates anew each year.

The NCCB foresaw that some bishops might prefer to reserve the confirmation of non-infants for themselves, even if pastors baptize them. But the National Statutes say that if a bishop wants to confirm any such persons, he should baptize them as well:

> A diocesan bishop who is desirous of confirming neophytes should reserve to himself the baptism of adults.[54]

"Neophytes" are the newly baptized.

This statute again demonstrates how closely the model of adult initiation views the sacraments of confirmation and baptism: They need each other to express the fullness of the paschal mystery.

Symbols of the Rite

The rite of confirmation is filled with symbols which express the meaning of the sacrament.

The **place** of confirmation: Confirmation should take place "either at the baptismal font or in the sanctuary, depending on the place where . . . baptism has been celebrated."[55] It takes place where baptism takes place. The location itself shows the interrelationship of these two sacraments.

Hands outstretched: "The celebrant holds his hands outstretched over the entire group of those to be confirmed."[56] This takes place as he recites the prayer for the gift of the Holy Spirit. The gesture is significant because in most prayers, the celebrant stands with his hands lifted up; here they are stretched out over the group. In the liturgy outstretched hands generally signify that the prayer asks for a blessing or for the coming of the Holy Spirit.

Chrism: As explained above, chrism signifies both Jesus and the Spirit. Those being confirmed now share in the role of Jesus Christ—priest, prophet, and king; and the Holy Spirit's presence is marked by the consecrated oil. When priests assist the bishop in confirmation, he actually hands the chrism to them,[57] a sign that it is the bishop's role to pray for the consecration of chrism, and that the priests extend the bishop's ministry.

Chrism is applied on the forehead with the sign of the cross. Those to be confirmed are sealed, or "branded" with the sign of eternal life. They are marked as members of Christ's body and share in his paschal mystery and mission.

Godparents: Those to be confirmed are accompanied by godparents. These are the same godparents who accompanied them moments before in baptism, again linking these sacraments.[58] The sponsors represent the Christian community, the body of Christ, in which those to be confirmed are new members. Their gesture, placing their right hand on the shoulder of the candidate, demonstrates their role of support.

Song: During confirmation a song may be sung which explains the meaning of the rite and unifies the community of believers in one voice.[59] This is the community these candidates have just joined.

The **name**: The candidate's name is spoken as the priest or bishop applies the chrism. "N., be sealed with the Gift of the Holy Spirit."[60] The use of the name recalls the importance of the name in the rites leading up to and including baptism. Catechumens are called by name as they pass from stage to stage;[61] they even enroll their names in a special book as part of their preparation for baptism.[62] As the waters of baptism pour over them, they hear the minister calling them by name again: "N., I baptize you in the name of the Father, and of the Son, and of the Holy Spirit."[63] The name is the Christian name. To call the baptized by their name is to call them Christian. So this too is a symbol which unites confirmation with baptism.

Formerly, confirmation imitated baptism by asking the candidates for a new name. Now it honors baptism by keeping the baptismal name.

The **peace**: The minister who anoints the foreheads of the candidates adds, "Peace be with you."[64] The greeting of peace is a hallmark of Christian life. Christians exchange peace before receiving communion as a sign of their bond of love. At a typical Mass, catechumens are dismissed to reflect on the Scriptures after the homily and before the assembly extends the sign of peace. Giving peace is a symbol that these newly confirmed candidates share full communion with the Catholic family.

Sprinkling: The newly confirmed take their places with the assembly to which they now belong, and all are sprinkled with the waters of baptism which unite them in the mystery of Christ.[65]

Concerns

The meaning of confirmation in adult initiation should be clear from its proximity to baptism:

> the unity of the paschal mystery, the close link between the mission of the Son and the outpouring of the Holy Spirit, and the connection between the two sacraments through which the Son and the Holy Spirit come with the Father to those who are baptized.[66]

The whole model should affirm a unity of purpose, flowing from history and theology. It should, but it still suffers some inconsistencies.

The Age of Adulthood: It seems clear from the writings quoted above that "catechetical age" is about the time in which canon law says children "have attained the use of reason."[67] Commenting on the rites of Christian initiation, the order does not further specify what "catechetical age" is, since it will vary from child to child.

So it's surprising to find the order of Christian initiation of adults suggesting that the bishop preside at the Vigil "at least for the initiation of those who are fourteen years old or older."[68]

After the principle has been established that children of catechetical age are to be treated as adults, the intrusion of a separate class of initiates at age fourteen is surprising. Is it because those younger than fourteen should follow the rite of infant baptism? Is fourteen the real catechetical age? Are bishops less capable of presiding at a lengthy Vigil liturgy for children under age fourteen?

The origins of this instruction seem to come from the code of canon law. Not the current one, but the code of 1917. There, canon 744 suggests that the baptism "of adults" may be referred to the bishop. The current code expands on this expression: "The baptism of adults, at least those who have completed fourteen years of age, is to be referred to the bishop."[69]

Where does the notion come from that adults are those who have reached fourteen years of age? From early Roman law which set adulthood at puberty. A remnant of the influence of this law is found today in a canon on marriage which states,

> A man before he has completed his sixteenth year of age, and likewise a woman before she has completed her fourteenth year of age, cannot enter a valid marriage.[70]

Thus, in specifying at what age one becomes an adult, the order of Christian initiation of adults has confused the status of "catechetical age" and raised the question why this should be important in the matter of whom the bishop should baptize.

The Time of Confirmation: After the principle has been established that confirmation should follow baptism in this model except for grave reasons, the order of Christian initiation of adults admits that in certain cases when there is serious reason, confirmation may be postponed until near the end of the period of post-baptismal catechesis, for example, Pentecost Sunday.[71]

This passage then refers the reader to the following instruction:

To close the period of postbaptismal catechesis, some sort of celebration should be held at the end of the Easter season near Pentecost Sunday; festivities in keeping with local custom may accompany the occasion.[72]

But is "some sort of celebration" confirmation? Under what "certain cases," and with whose "local custom"?

It is difficult to reconcile these instructions with the statement that adults are not to be baptized without receiving confirmation immediately afterward, because the conjunction of the two celebrations signifies the unity of the paschal mystery.[73]

Post-Baptismal Anointing: In the rite of infant baptism, after pouring the water, priests or deacons may anoint the crown of the infant's head with chrism. (This differs from confirmation, where chrism is applied to the forehead.) The presider explains that the rite unites the newly baptized to the body of Christ, who is priest, prophet, and king.

This rite is omitted when confirmation follows baptism immediately. It is included for adults only if confirmation is separated from baptism.

Why this is so is not clear. It seems to admit that confirmation has taken over the meaning of this anointing. This is partly why confirmation seems to carry more than one meaning: It is both an outpouring of the Holy Spirit and a joining to the membership of Christ. These meanings surely fit together, but the extra symbolism makes the point of confirmation less clear. Further, in the case of the infant, why retain the post-baptismal anointing at all if the child is to be confirmed later?

Vatican Council II asked for the simplification of the rites of the church—eliminating duplications so that the meaning would be more evident. Here is a case where the simplification of the rite of anointing—omitting it for catechumens only—may have confused its meaning.

Laying On of Hands: The rite calls the prayer of confirmation the "Laying On of Hands."[74] This is not quite correct. The celebrant holds his hands outstretched over those to be confirmed. He does not actually touch them with his hands.[75]

This is an unfortunate oversight. Outstretched hands may seem to be a way to "lay hands" on a large number of people all at once, but it poorly substitutes for the more personal gesture which can be traced to the early church and to the Scriptures.

Omitting Confirmation: This is less an inconsistency as it is a point to be noted. As important as confirmation is for the full celebration of initiation and the symbolic expression of redemption, occasions arise when it is omitted.

If a catechumen's death is imminent, a priest may celebrate baptism alone. Of the sacraments of initiation, it is most important to baptize; confirming simply does not matter as much.

If no priest is available, ministers of communion or baptism do not confirm, but the church does not seem to mind much, since the celebrations of baptism and eucharist are more important. This goes to show that as exalted a place as confirmation holds among the rites of the church, it always bows to baptism.

2

Chrismation

Introduction

The model of confirmation in the previous chapter springs largely from documentation the Roman Catholic Church published in the 1970's. However, churches of the Eastern Rites have been following confirmation traditions that date back to the earliest Christian centuries. These churches use the word "chrismation" for what the Roman Rite calls "confirmation." Their perspective on chrismation, its place in initiation, and its manner of celebration are unique and important for a complete understanding of the sacrament.

This chapter will describe who the Eastern Rites are, how their tradition of infant chrismation originated, what chrismation means, and how it differs from baptism.

The Eastern Rites

Who are these Eastern Rites? The Eastern Rites are families of churches originating from cities which geographically lie east of the ancient Roman Empire and follow an oriental spirituality and way of thought. It helps to think of them in four families. The first is the Oriental Orthodox, a communion of five ancient churches of the east: Armenian, Coptic (Egyptian), Ethiopian, Syrian ("Jacobite"), and Malankar (Indian). They did not accept the teachings of the Council of Chalcedon in 451 regarding the nature of Christ. The second group is the Assyrian church, which adopted the Christology of Nestorius in 484, contrary to the teaching of the Roman church. A third group is the Orthodox church, embracing the patriarchates of Constantinople, Alexandria, Antioch, Jerusalem, and Moscow. They and the Roman church separated during the great schism of 1054. The fourth group is the Eastern Catholics in full communion with the church of Rome. Its largest family—including the Greek, Melkite, Russian, and Ruthenian Rites—is called Byzantine, and stems from Constantinople. Christians in these places of origin developed their own spirituality, liturgy, and theology in the first few centuries after Christ, and their customs have endured to this day.[76]

All these churches are related. To use the family analogy, one may think of them as individual families all joined to each other as cousins down the family tree. One of those cousins is the Roman Catholic Church, or the church of the west, also called "the Latin Rite." All families endure tension, and these "ritual families" were no exception. Still, in the beginning all these families co-existed in better harmony.

Serious problems arose in the eleventh century. Differences in liturgical matters between east and west caused the leaders of each to ask the others to conform. Old wounds reopened, communications were mistranslated, blunders were made, and churches east and west simply severed their union.

Since that time, some healing has happened, but today the many Eastern Rites fall into two basic groups: those who are in union with Rome, and those who are not. They are called "Catholic" and "Orthodox" respectively. Neither group receives communion at the other group's eucharist. Attempts at reunion have yet to bear fruit. But since all Eastern Rites share the same origins with the west, the Roman Catholic Church recognizes all the sacraments of the Eastern Rites, whether they are Catholic or Orthodox. The Orthodox, however, recognize none of the Catholic sacraments except baptism. Hopes for complete reunion run stronger since the advances of Vatican Council II.

For the most part, the liturgy of chrismation developed in these Rites long before the eleventh century schism. So all the churches of the east share similar ideas about chrismation. Although there are some variations from one Rite to another, they have so much in common that this chapter treats them all in a unit as a distinct model of confirmation.

How Chrismation Is Done

In every Eastern Church the rite of baptism always includes the rite of chrismation. It is never deferred from initiation. The priest who baptizes also chrismates with oil consecrated by the bishop, or "patriarch."

Vatican II's *Decree on the Catholic Eastern Churches* affirmed this custom:

> The established practice with regard to the minister of Confirmation, which has existed among Eastern Christians from ancient times, is to be fully restored. Accordingly priests are able to confer this sacrament, using chrism blessed by their patriarch or bishop.[77]

In fact, priests of any Catholic Rite may confer this sacrament on any Catholic:

> All priests of an Eastern Rite can confer this sacrament validly, either in conjunction with baptism or separately, on all the faithful of any Rite, including the Latin Rite. For liceity, however, they must follow what is laid down by their common and particular canon law. Priests also of the Latin Rite, in accordance with the faculties which they have in regard to the administration of this sacrament, may administer it also to the faithful of the Eastern Churches, without prejudice to the Rite. For liceity they must follow the prescriptions of common and particular canon law.[78]

That means any priest may confirm, even in a Rite different from his own, but he should follow the rules of the Rite.

There are two occasions when chrismation is administered apart from baptism. Both involve receiving someone into an Eastern Rite church. In one instance, the person being received comes from a church which does not recognize confirmation as a sacrament—for example, from any of the churches of the Reform. The other instance is when someone joins the Eastern Rite from the Roman Catholic Church—if that person was baptized, but his or her confirmation was deferred.[79] For example, if a Roman Catholic family decides to join a Byzantine Rite, a six year old in that family who was baptized as an infant, but has not yet been confirmed in the Roman Rite, would be chrismated in the Byzantine Rite when the family joins.

Chrismation rituals are not the same among all the churches of the east. This is because they developed their traditions independently by region and guarded them with pride. For example, the Nestorians impose hands on the candidates but use no oil. The Greeks anoint with chrism but do not impose hands. The Jacobite and uniate Syrians of Antioch impose hands and then anoint with chrism. The Ethiopians anoint several parts of the body with oil first and then impose hands on the candidates. The Copts do the same for them and then place a crown on their heads. Catholic Armenians impose hands before anointing with chrism; Orthodox Armenians omit the imposition of hands.[80]

This chapter will focus on the formulas of the Byzantine Rite, since the churches of that family are most numerous. "Official texts" for this Rite do not exist in English in the same way they do for the Roman Rite. Various translations of the original Slavonic and Greek are available.[81]

The Byzantine Rite of the Catholic Church celebrates chrismation as part of baptism. After the pouring of the water, the newly baptized receive a white cloth and a lighted candle—symbols of their new life in Christ. The chrismation follows.

The priest begins with a prayer of thanksgiving, blessing God for the mystery of salvation, and for sharing it with the faithful through the cleansing and sanctification of baptism and chrismation. Praising God for the rebirth of the newly baptized, the prayer makes this request:

> O Master and Most Merciful King of all, grant him (her) also the Seal of the Gift of Your Holy, Almighty, and Adorable Spirit and the partaking of the most Holy Body and Precious Blood of Christ, Your Anointed One. Keep him (her) in Your sanctification, and strengthen him (her) in the Catholic Faith.

Deliver him (her) from the Evil One and from all his cunning, and through a salutary fear of You preserve his (her) soul in purity and in righteousness, so that he (she) may please You in his (her) every word and deed, and thus may become a son (daughter) and heir to Your Heavenly Kingdom.[82]

Then the priest dips his thumb into the chrism and traces the sign of the cross on the forehead, eyes, nostrils, mouth, ears, breast, hands, and feet of the newly baptized, saying, "The Seal of the Gift ✚ of the Holy Spirit."[83]

Thus, the ritual calls chrismation the "seal of the gift of the Holy Spirit," and the prayer asks that the one chrismated be strengthened in faith and delivered from evil.

Eucharist follows chrismation in accordance with the code of Oriental law.[84] The Eastern Rites preserve the ancient tradition of offering eucharist even to infants in the complete rites of initiation.

Chrismation itself is better understood in context with another ritual, the consecration of chrism. In the east, the newly baptized symbolize their membership in the larger church community through the anointing with chrism consecrated not by the local priest, but by the senior bishop or patriarch of the entire church. Both rituals, chrismation and the consecration of chrism, together form the liturgical basis for the anointing.

The consecration of chrism takes place once a year, usually during lent. The patriarch presides over the gathering of bishops or hierarchs, and the chrism from this single consecration is distributed throughout the world. Each year some of the old chrism is added to the newly consecrated chrism. So whenever a new Christian is chrismated, he or she participates in the unity of the church in all the world and in all time.[85]

The prayer for the consecration of chrism begins by recalling the ancient scriptural tradition of chrism:

Lord of mercy and Father of lights, from whom comes every good work and perfect gift, grant us, though unworthy, the grace necessary to serve this great and enlivening Mystery as You gave it to Your servant Moses, Your servant Samuel and Your holy apostles.[86]

The prayer then calls on the Holy Spirit to sanctify the chrism, which will protect and sanctify in the sacraments of today as it was prefigured in the traditions of old:

> Send your Holy Spirit upon this chrism. Make of it a royal and spiritual unction, protector of life, sanctifier of souls and bodies, an oil of gladness prefigured in the law, shining forth in the New Testament. For through it were anointed priests, prophets and kings: through it You Yourself anointed Your holy apostles and all those born anew in the bath of regeneration at their hands and those of their successors, the priests and bishops unto this very day.[87]

The prayer then asks God to make the chrism a perfect seal to baptism. The function of chrism will be to seal the baptized as members of the family of God, preserved in and recognized for their holiness. Thus although chrism has many uses in east and west, this prayer focuses on its role in chrismation:

> Yes, Lord God Almighty, by the coming of Your holy and adorable Spirit, make of it a garment of incorruptibility, a perfect seal that imprints on those who receive Your divine Bath the right to hear Your godly Name and that of Your only Son and Your Holy Spirit, so as to be known by You, to be members of Your family, Your fellow-citizens, Your servants and handmaids, so they may be sanctified of all sin by putting on again the vesture of Your spotless glory—that they may be recognized thanks to this divine sign, by Your holy angels and archangels and all the heavenly powers that they might terrify all the wicked and foul demons.[88]

Sealed with chrism, the baptized will bear Christ in their hearts. They become the dwelling place of God:

> They will become Your own people, a royal priesthood, a holy nation, stamped with the seal of Your spotless chrism, they will bear Christ in their hearts as Your dwelling place, O God and Father, in the Holy Spirit, through ages of ages. For You are holy, O our God, and You rest among the holy, and we

send up glory to You, Father, Son and Holy Spirit, now and always and forever and ever.[89]

Thus the prayer for the consecration of chrism keeps the newly-baptized in the forefront. It is for them that this oil is consecrated. Not only is chrismation firmly linked to baptism, but the very consecration of chrism is as well.

Origins of Chrismation

The Eastern Rites differ from the Roman Rite with regard to the minister of chrismation and the usual occasion for it. In the east the ordinary minister is the priest who baptizes, and the occasion is baptism, regardless of the age of the new Christian. The Roman Rite follows this procedure only for those baptized after catechetical age; it defers confirmation for those baptized in infancy. In the west, the bishop is the ordinary minister and confirmation is separated from baptism by many years.

History shows why these two practices diverged in the same Church.

The Scriptures record many instances when the Holy Spirit is invoked through an imposition of hands. The apostles imposed hands on new followers of Christ.[90] Many passages in the epistles refer to the sending and receiving of the Holy Spirit,[91] or the seal of the Spirit.[92] Although these passages may carry images of initiation, they predate the development of confirmation as a post-baptismal ritual. It is therefore improper to call them "confirmation texts"; there is no confirmation as such in the Bible. All that is clear is that from apostolic times the reception of the Holy Spirit could be symbolized through a common gesture, the imposition of hands, although in at least one instance, baptism *followed* the reception of the Spirit.[93]

In the first few centuries after Christ, the earliest ancestor among liturgical texts for confirmation is the *Apostolic Tradition* of Hippolytus, composed around 215 A.D. Hippolytus was a Roman priest, antipope, and saint who composed many treatises and homilies. The *Apostolic Tradition* contains an early record of how eucharist and baptism were celebrated in the early church. According to Hippolytus, a priest gives a post-baptismal anointing at the font, and then the newly baptized are brought to the bishop for the imposition of his hand[94] and another anointing with chrism. From this text and other sources it seems clear that this ritual of sealing after baptism was performed by the bishop.[95]

This anointing by the bishop, attested in many early documents, became the forerunner of confirmation. The term "confirmation" still did not occur,[96] but the ritual was beginning to take shape after baptism and before eucharist.[97]

It soon became difficult for the bishop to anoint everyone at the Easter Vigil. Converts to Christianity were too numerous; bishops were too few. The Western Church began to allow the imposition of hands to be deferred to a time when the bishop could remain its minister. The Council of Elvira in 305 suggested that any member of the faithful may baptize sick catechumens. If the new Christians got better, they were to be brought to the bishop for the imposition of hands.[98] The Council of Orange in 441 allowed priests who received sick heretics to the church to sign them with chrism if no bishop was present.[99] These permissions assume that the bishop ordinarily performed the anointing or imposition of hands after baptism.

Further, Christianity spread so quickly that adult baptisms declined as infant baptisms rose. Augustine's doctrine on original sin influenced the early baptism of babies, and a growing privatization of spirituality in the early Middle Ages accompanied the loss of community participation in the preparation of new members for the church. The catechumenate disappeared. And the west, desiring to keep the bishop's role in anointing the baptized, summarily deferred that ritual to a later celebration when the bishop could come.

In the east permissions for a priest to anoint with chrism were unnecessary since priests customarily completed the rites of baptism themselves, including chrismation, but without the imposition of hands. It seems likely that the origins of chrismation lie with a ritual that included an imposition of hands by the bishop.[100] But when priests became the ordinary minister, they abandoned the imposition of hands as the gesture reserved to the bishop, and kept the anointing of chrism.[101] After all, chrism had to be consecrated by a bishop, and its usage brought the role of the absent bishop into the baptismal liturgy.

In the west the anointing gradually took on the name "confirmation," since the bishop "confirmed" the priest's baptism. The term first appears in several councils of fifth century Gaul[102] and in a homily attributed to Faustus of Riez or Eusebius Gallicanus.[103] This homily interpreted the separation of confirmation from baptism to indicate that confirmation strengthened Christians for spiritual struggles; it regarded confirmation more as a sacrament of Christian maturity than one tied to baptismal initiation. In the eighth century this same homily found its way into a collection of documents where it was falsely attributed to the early fourth century Pope Melchiades.[104] The "new" author gave the text much more authority than it had before, and the west firmly attached a theology of Christian maturity to confirmation.

Thus, the practice of confirmation/chrismation diverged west and east. In the west, the minister was the bishop, and the candidate was more often someone who had been baptized many years before. In the east, the minister was the priest, and the occasion was baptism. They held in common the connection between anointing and the Holy Spirit. But in the west, the anointing symbolized an outpouring of the gifts of the Holy Spirit. In the east, the anointing more often symbolized the seal of the Holy Spirit on those newly baptized. Practically, however, the meaning remained the same: confirmation/chrismation gives the Holy Spirit.

What Chrismation Means

The key to understanding eastern chrismation is in the word itself: chrism. This ancient oil, a mixture of olive oil, wine, balsam, and some forty perfumes, is a sacred symbol of the Holy Spirit. In the patriarch's consecration of chrism each year, this oil is endowed with a special presence of the Holy Spirit. In the fourth century, Cyril of Jerusalem actually compared this to the presence of Christ in the eucharist:

> After the invocation of the Holy Spirit, the eucharistic bread is no longer mere bread, but the body of Christ. In the same way this holy chrism is no longer a mere common ointment after the invocation. It is the gift of Christ, imparting his divinity by the presence of the Holy Spirit.[105]

The anointing of chrism, then, symbolizes the presence of the Holy Spirit. This kind of symbolization is recognized in many ways in the Eastern Churches; for example, the Gospels symbolize the presence of Christ; and icons symbolize the presence of the one represented.[106]

Chrismation also symbolizes the seal of the Spirit. Following the water bath of baptism, anointing with oil symbolically "seals" the new Christian, and completes the work of baptism.[107]

The seal marks a sign of ownership. It protects one from violation. It guarantees the agreement. Giving this seal in the form of a cross indicates that chrismation "brands" one as the property of Christ.[108]

Chrismation implicitly carries the purpose of preparing one for receiving the eucharist. Because baptism and chrismation are two parts of the same ritual, together they form the entrance into the sacramental life of the church. One does not approach the other sacraments, especially the eucharist, without having first celebrated baptism and chrismation.

The code of Oriental law suggests that eucharist be given to new Christians as soon as possible:

> Sacramental initiation into the mystery of salvation is completed with the reception of the Divine Eucharist. Therefore, the Divine Eucharist is administered to the faithful Christian as soon as possible after baptism and chrismation of the holy oil, according to the norm of the particular law of each autonomous church.[109]

This includes giving communion to infants.

> Concerning the participation of infants in the Divine Eucharist after baptism and chrismation of holy oil—when the proper precautions are taken, the rules of the liturgical books of each autonomous church are maintained.[110]

For the Byzantine family, this means that communion is to be offered in every instance of initiation, including the case of infants. The prayer of chrismation explicitly asks God to grant the newly baptized a participation in the eucharist. However, not all Byzantine churches follow this practice for infants. Many defer eucharist to a later age. Offering eucharist at initiation more clearly reveals the preparatory nature of chrismation.

Chrismation carries implications for the Christian life. Surely it is the gift of God's Holy Spirit, but in marking the faithful as Christians it expects them to pattern their lives after the model of Christ. Because chrismation seals the Christian in baptism, it opens the door to the lifelong responsibility of Christianity. Through commitment and catechesis, Christians foster continual spiritual growth. Chrismation, then, presumes that its catechesis will nurture fidelity to the Christian way of life.[111]

It is the Holy Spirit who makes this spiritual growth possible. The Holy Spirit is not only the gift in chrismation, the Spirit is the agent of chrismation. All God's work is accomplished through the Holy Spirit, and chrismation is no exception.[112] The ritual implies this in its spare language. When the priest anoints the newly baptized with chrism, he says simply, "The seal of the gift of the Holy Spirit." He does not say, "I seal you," but simply proclaims the reality. It is the Spirit who acts.

Chrismation, then, has this meaning: Through chrismation, the Holy Spirit seals the newly baptized in Christ, preparing them for eucharist and for the demands of the Christian life.

Relationship Between Chrismation and Baptism

Calling chrismation a sacrament separate from baptism is accurate, but the distinction came from the west's influence. The Roman Rite did not fix the number of sacraments at seven until after Peter Lombard wrote his *Sentences* in the twelfth century. Essentially, no one had asked, "How many sacraments are there?" prior to that time. Lombard called confirmation a separate sacrament because by that time it was being celebrated as a separate event in the west. No such separation had happened in the east, but to maintain the same sacraments with the west, the east numbered chrismation as a sacrament separate from baptism, even though they have always been celebrated together.

The difficulty then is to distinguish how the Holy Spirit comes in confirmation/chrismation, since the Spirit was already given in baptism. The temptation is to quantify the gift of the Spirit, to say the newly baptized receive "more" Spirit in confirmation/chrismation, but one cannot quantify God.

Still, the liturgy and the Christian life assume that "growth" will take place within the faithful. Although God remains the same, participation in and appreciation of God may increase.

Since baptism and chrismation occur together, this distinction of participation in the Holy Spirit is largely academic. But the point will be important to remember that for the Eastern Churches, chrismation marks the seal of the Spirit in baptism. It does not mark a formal acceptance of Christianity or achievement of spiritual maturity that is different from that marked by baptism. Consequently, the literature of the Roman Rite describing confirmation as a delayed sacrament of maturity or commitment is not applicable to the entire Eastern Church.

In the east, chrismation is offered to adults, children, and infants alike. When adults are baptized and chrismated, they symbolize their conversion and commitment to Christ. When children are baptized and chrismated, they enter the mystery of Christ which will continue to unfold throughout their lives.[113]

> *Chrismation* is not so much the second mystery, as it is the very fulfillment of baptism. While baptism incorporates us into Christ's new risen existence, *chrismation* makes us partakers of his Spirit, the very source of this new life and of total illumination.[114]

Concerns

The Eastern Churches follow most closely the earliest historical precedents for chrismation: They celebrate it as part of the baptismal rite of initiation. In spite of its antiquity, this model still raises some concerns.

First is the unanimous practice in the Byzantine Rite which

did not preserve the imposition of hands in the sacrament. (This custom actually influenced the Roman Rite's practice and theology of confirmation as well.) The symbolism of chrism is rich, but the absence of the imposition of hands is regrettable. Its origins as a symbol for the coming of the Holy Spirit can be traced to apostolic times, and its usage in early initiation rituals is well-documented.

Second, in confirmation the Roman Rite developed a sacrament which marked the physical and spiritual maturity of children baptized in infancy. Since the Eastern Rites never developed such a ritual for catechetical development, are they poorer for it? Is there a place for a rite of maturity? The sacrament of reconciliation partially fills that need with its emphasis on continued conversion, but the Roman Rite has long distinguished catechetical achievement from repentance.

Finally, the Eastern Rites celebrate one anointing instead of the two recorded by Hippolytus: after pouring water the third century priest anointed the newly-baptized, and then the bishop anointed again while imposing a hand on the new Christian. The priest in the east who baptizes also chrismates; there is no second anointing. Is this a simplification, or just a different tradition? Could two anointings better represent separate meanings; one, perhaps, a participation in Christ, the other the seal of the Spirit? The Roman Rite preserved both anointings for those baptized in infancy. The divergent practices cloud the meaning of the two anointings.

The many Eastern Churches have deep traditions that distinguish one from another. Such traditions do not and should not change lightly. But their meaning should be rich and clear.

3

Protestant–Anglican Churches

Introduction

Confirmation belongs not to the Catholic Church alone. Several other faiths also celebrate the rite. However, although there is one baptism among the many Christian churches, there are many confirmations, and the rite's meaning changes among them.

This chapter will examine the confirmation rites in several churches of the Protestant and Anglican traditions. The faiths which could be treated here are many in number; only a few must suffice. Selections are from those which have printed national materials for the ritual, a commentary, and/or principles in church law.[115] Several large Christian bodies do not celebrate any form of confirmation, nor do they have printed materials even governing baptism on a national level. Most such denominations baptize with water in the name of the Trinity, but the practice is rooted in Scripture and common oral tradition, not legislation.

Before examining the contemporary practice, some history may help.

History

Martin Luther was not the first to challenge the practice of confirmation, but his thorough treatment covered more ground and received more attention than other ones.[116] The earliest Church Fathers all called certain rites of the church "sacraments," but no one counted an exact number of sacraments until Peter

Lombard in the twelfth century. Peter's system went unchallenged until John Wycliffe and John Hus questioned it in the fourteenth and fifteenth centuries. Their critique caused some controversy and gained many followers, but it paled before the influence of Martin Luther.

Confirmation was formally recognized as a sacrament in the Middle Ages. By that time it had already drifted from its initial moorings in the rites of initiation, and had become an independent celebration. Luther's critique of confirmation, then, pertained to a sacrament which resembled a maturity ritual more than initiation into the church.

Luther's most extensive treatment of confirmation comes from his classic treatise, *On the Babylonian Captivity of the Church*. There he redefined "sacraments" on principles based on baptism and eucharist. Both baptism and eucharist may be found in the Scriptures with a promise and a sign from Jesus. But none of the other "sacraments" can boast the same. Consequently, Luther recognized only these two as true sacraments in the church, the others as sacramental rituals.

Confirmation, then, according to Luther, is not a sacrament. Confirmation faced no greater challenge in the late Middle Ages. Luther did not argue the proper age of the recipient, nor the meaning of the ritual. Rather he challenged its very essence as a sacrament in the church. Luther objected to the practice—he denounced confirmation as a "not too burdensome rite to adorn the office of bishops," so that "they may not be entirely without work in the Church."[117] Still, in a later work, he valued the idea "that every pastor might investigate the faith from children and if it be good and sincere, he may impose hands and confirm."[118] But this was to be a pious rite, not a sacrament.

Luther was joined by other Reformers, and confirmation developed throughout their churches and ultimately in the Anglican communion as a rite noting a child's achievement of a level of catechesis—in short, a maturity rite.

Contemporary Practice

The practice of confirmation remains strong in many Protestant and Anglican churches. Some differences are noted below.

The Lutheran Church

Confirmation in the Evangelical Lutheran Church in America has been recommended for tenth grade.[119] It fills one of several occasions now entitled "Affirmation of Baptism." The *Lutheran Book of Worship* describes confirmation as follows:

> Confirmation marks the completion of the congregation's program of confirmation ministry, a period of instruction in the Christian faith as confessed in the teachings of the Lutheran Church. Those who have completed this program were made members of the Church in Baptism. Confirmation includes a public profession of faith into which the candidates were baptized, thus underscoring God's action in their Baptism.[120]

Several points are noteworthy:

1. Confirmation involves the **community**; it is the congregation's program of ministry.
2. It concludes a period of Christian **instruction** in the Lutheran Church.
3. Its **candidates** were all baptized as Lutherans. Those joining the Lutheran Church from another denomination celebrate "Reception into Membership," not confirmation.
4. A public **confession of faith** is included. Candidates are expected to demonstrate their faith with their own voice.
5. This confession underscores **God's action in baptism**. As infants the candidates could not profess their own faith. Still, baptism initiated them into the body of Christ because of God's action. This public confession of their own faith demonstrates that God acted in their baptism as infants.

The Affirmation of Baptism covers three circumstances: confirmation of those baptized and instructed, reception into membership of those belonging to other denominations, and restoration to membership for those who have drifted from active participation. In all three instances, the candidates publicly profess their faith (a parallel to the "renewal of baptismal promises" in the Catholic rite). Intercessions follow. Then the minister asks this question:

Do you intend to continue in the covenant God made with you in Holy Baptism: to live among God's faithful people, to hear his Word and share in his supper, to proclaim the good news of God in Christ through word and deed, to serve all people, following the example of our Lord Jesus, and to strive for justice and peace in all the earth?[121]

Thus the candidates are asked specifically about the demands of the baptismal covenant. Their willingness to remain faithful to it establishes their preparedness for confirmation and the other forms of affirmation of baptism. The prayer which follows, paraphrasing Isaiah, resembles the prayer in the Catholic rite of confirmation:

Gracious Lord, through water and the Spirit you have made these *men and women* your own. You forgave them all their sins and brought them to newness of life. Continue to strengthen them with the Holy Spirit, and daily increase in them your gifts of grace: the spirit of wisdom and understanding, the spirit of counsel and might, the spirit of knowledge and the fear of the Lord, the spirit of joy in your presence; through Jesus Christ, your Son, our Lord.[122]

Then the minister lays both hands on the head of each person and says,

Father in heaven, for Jesus' sake, stir up in _____ the gift of your Holy Spirit; confirm *his/her* faith, guide *his/her* life, empower *him/her* in *his/her* serving, give *him/her* patience in suffering, and bring *him/her* to everlasting life.[123]

Thus, confirmation signifies the stirring up of and increase in the gifts of the Holy Spirit.

It helps to compare this with the Lutheran rite of baptism. There, after the sponsors confess the faith of the church for the child, and after the water has been poured, a ritual follows, significant for the study of confirmation. The minister lays both hands on the head of each of the baptized and prays for the Holy Spirit:

God, the Father of our Lord Jesus Christ, we give you thanks for freeing your sons and daughters from the power of sin and for raising them up to a new life through this holy sacrament.

Pour your Holy Spirit upon _____: the spirit of wisdom and understanding, the spirit of counsel and might, the spirit of knowledge and the fear of the Lord, the spirit of joy in your presence.[124]

This prayer differs from the affirmation of baptism, the Holy Spirit is given here in baptism; in confirmation, the same gifts are called forth again in a prayer which recalls the one at the baptism. The difference is that the prayer at baptism asks for a first gift of the Spirit ("Pour your Holy Spirit upon _____"), and the prayer at confirmation asks for a strengthening of that original gift ("Continue to strengthen them with the Holy Spirit, and daily increase in them your gifts of grace").

Then the minister marks the sign of the cross on the forehead of each of the baptized. He or she may do so with oil. This new addition to the Lutheran rite imitates Catholic confirmation in the model of adult initiation: signing the forehead with oil immediately after baptism. The minister says, "_____, child of God, you have been sealed by the Holy Spirit and marked with the cross of Christ forever."[125]

In the past Lutherans understood confirmation in many ways:

Confirmation has been seen as a time of instruction in the essentials of the faith as set forth in (Luther's) *Small Catechism*. It has been seen as a means of church discipline by which one surrenders oneself to Christ and submits to the church's rule. It has been seen as a quasi-sacrament which added to Baptism the fuller presence of the Holy Spirit and which bestowed church membership on the recipient who now was entitled to receive Holy Communion and enter upon the undefined "spiritual privileges" of the church. It has been seen as the subjective acceptance of Christ as personal Lord, a decisive conversion experience. It has been understood as the completion of an educational course, a kind of graduation ceremony.[126]

Catholics are not alone in their confusion. But in 1970 the Joint Commission on the Theology and Practice of Confirmation defined confirmation as follows:

Confirmation is a pastoral and educational ministry of the church which helps the baptized child through Word and Sacrament to identify more deeply with the Christian community and participate more fully in its mission.[127]

Lutheran confirmation may be repeated, whenever members feel the need to celebrate it again.

(Confirmation) is an affirmation of Baptism, a way of saying "Yes" to Baptism. It is not therefore an unrepeatable, once-for-all act but something that can be done at several points in one's life.[128]

It is not required for first communion, "for the gift of Communion is the birthright of the baptized."[129]

The Lutherans have settled the confirmation question by making it a ritual for maturity in the Christian faith, in which the gift of the Holy Spirit, received at baptism, is now stirred up and increased.

The Lutheran Church—Missouri Synod produced its own service book in 1982.[130] It does not divide "Affirmation of Baptism" as does the *Lutheran Book of Worship*. Rather, confirmation stands as its own ritual. It begins with a confession of faith and a statement of intention to continue in the church's confession. The minister reads the confirmation text while laying hands upon each member's head:

_____, God the Father of our Lord Jesus Christ, give you his Holy Spirit, the Spirit of wisdom and knowledge, of grace and prayer, of power and strength, of sanctification and the fear of God.[131]

Then the minister says,

Upon this your profession and promise I invite and welcome you, as members of the Evangelical Lutheran Church and of this congregation, to share with us in all the gifts our Lord has for his Church and to live them out continually in his worship and service.[132]

A prayer of thanksgiving concludes the service, praying that the newly confirmed "may continue steadfast and victorious to the day when all who have fought the good fight of faith shall receive the crown of righteousness."[133]

The Missouri Synod's confirmation prayer asks for "the Holy Spirit," where the Evangelical Lutheran Church in America's confirmation prayer asks for a "daily increase" in the "gifts of grace." The Missouri Synod's texts imply that church membership comes with confirmation; the Evangelical Lutheran Church in America's imply that it came with baptism.

In the baptismal rite of the Missouri Synod there is no prayer for the sevenfold gift of the Spirit inspired by Isaiah. That prayer accompanies confirmation only. This parallels the Roman Catholic tradition. (The Evangelical Lutheran Church in America offers this prayer in both places.) No anointing or prayer of sealing follows the pouring of water. Instead, the minister lays his hand on the newly baptized and says,

> Almighty God, the Father of our Lord Jesus Christ, who has given you the new birth of water and of the Spirit and has forgiven you all your sins, strengthen you with his grace to life everlasting. Peace be with you.[134]

Surely the confirmation rite of the Catholic Church inspired this prayer, with its plea for strengthening and its concluding sign of peace. But confirmation itself always comes long after baptism for a Missouri Synod Lutheran; indeed, for Lutherans in general.

The Presbyterian Church (U.S.A.)

Since 1980 the Presbyterian Church (U.S.A.) has been revising all its rituals for public worship. The publication of *Holy Baptism and Service for the Renewal of Baptism* reveals an achievement of much research and pastoral sensitivity.[135] This ritual was published for trial usage and its preparers welcome evaluations of the text.

As the title suggests, the work divides into two sections—one for baptism, the other for the renewal of baptism. In this second half Presbyterians find what they have traditionally called "confirmation" or "commissioning." However, it now carries the title "Public Profession of Faith." There is no service entitled "confirmation" as such, but this rite clearly parallels confirmation in other traditions.

The Presbyterians include six occasions for the renewal of baptism: Public Profession of Faith, Renewal of Baptism for Those Who Have Been Estranged from the Church, Renewal of Baptism for a Congregation, Renewal of Baptism Marking Occasions of Growth in Faith, Renewal of Baptism for the Sick and the Dying, and Renewal of Baptism in Pastoral Counseling.

The Public Profession of Faith is described as follows:

> It is the proper development from baptism, a claiming of the promises and responsibilities that baptism entails. Baptized children are part of the church, yet their response to God's grace leads to new roles within the congregation. In this sense this particular occasion of the renewal of baptism is a rite of passage from childhood to adulthood within the community of faith.[136]

Clearly, this public profession pertains to those baptized in infancy who now accept the faith and its responsibilities on their own. Other occasions may follow in life, when a member feels "a new sense of commitment, a new level of growth as a Christian, or a sense of calling to a particular ministry." Those circumstances may be ritualized in a similar ceremony, the Renewal of Baptism Marking Occasions of Growth in Faith. But the Public Profession of Faith seems to be an event that happens once.

The Constitution of the Presbyterian Church describes the occasion this way:

> The church nurtures those baptized as children and calls them to make public their personal profession of faith and their acceptance of responsibility in the life of the church. When these persons are ready, they shall be examined by the session.[137] After the session has received them as active members they shall be presented to the congregation during a service of public worship. In that service the church shall confirm them in their baptismal identity. They shall reaffirm the vows taken at Baptism by

a. professing their faith in Jesus Christ as Lord and Savior,

b. renouncing evil and affirming their reliance on God's grace,

c. declaring their intention to participate actively and responsibly in the worship and mission of the church.

They are commissioned for full participation in the mission and governance of the church, and are welcomed by the congregation.[138]

What does the ritual look like? After renouncing evil and confessing faith, the candidates hear these words from the minister:

You have publicly professed your faith. Do you intend to continue in the covenant God made with you in your baptism, to be a faithful member of this congregation, to share in its ministry through your prayers and gifts, your study and service, and so fulfill your calling to be a disciple of Jesus Christ?[139]

After the candidates respond, "I do," the minister prays:

Gracious God, through water and the Spirit you claimed *these* your *servants* as your own. You cleansed *them* of *their* sins, gave *them* new life, and bound *them* to your service. Renew in *them* the covenant you made in *their* baptism. Send *them* forth in the power of the Spirit to love and serve you with joy, and strive for justice and peace in all the earth, in the name of Jesus Christ our Lord.[140]

After this prayer, the candidates kneel and the minister lays both hands upon the head of each. The minister may mark the sign of the cross on the forehead of the candidate with oil as he or she says,

O Lord, uphold _____ by your Holy Spirit. Daily increase in (*him, her*) your gifts of grace: the spirit of wisdom and understanding, the spirit of counsel and might, the spirit of knowledge and the fear of the Lord, the spirit of joy in your presence, both now and forever.[141]

Or the following prayer:

Defend, O Lord, your servant _____ with your heavenly grace, that (*he, she*) may continue yours forever, and daily increase in your Holy Spirit more and more, until (*he, she*) comes to your everlasting kingdom.[142]

The minister concludes by saying,

Ever-living God, guard *these* your *servants* with your protecting hand, and let your Holy Spirit be with *them* forever. Lead *them* to know and obey your Word that *they* may serve you in this life and dwell with you in the life to come; through Jesus Christ our Lord.[143]

The ceremony concludes with the exchange of peace.

The other occasions for renewal of baptism borrow from these texts.

An examination of the ceremony of baptism puts these prayers in context. After pouring the water, the minister lays hands on the head of the one baptized and prays,

O Lord, uphold _____ by your Holy Spirit. Give (*him, her*) the spirit of wisdom and understanding, the spirit of counsel and might, the spirit of knowledge and the fear of the Lord, the spirit of joy in your presence, both now and forever.[144]

The minister may then trace oil in the sign of the cross on the forehead of the one baptized, saying,

_____, child of the covenant, you have been sealed by the Holy Spirit in baptism, and marked as Christ's own forever.[145]

Baptism, then, seals the new member in the Holy Spirit. The Public Profession of Faith (formerly "confirmation") prays for a "daily increase" in the gifts of that Spirit. By avoiding the term "confirmation," the Presbyterian Church (U.S.A.) withdraws from the argument over when confirmation happens, and includes two rituals which descend from the two aspects of confirmation in history: one a part of the rites of initiation, the other the member's achievement of a more mature status.

The optional use of oil is a new addition and opens the Presbyterian Church to participate in the more ancient Christian tradition of these rites.

Public Profession does not confer membership; baptism does. But the Constitution implies that "active members" apply for this ceremony and that it constitutes their eligibility for "full participation in the mission and governance of the church."

Further, although the ceremony is not called "confirmation," the Constitution acknowledges that in that service the church "confirms" the candidates in their baptismal identity.

The Episcopal Church

Q. What is Confirmation?
A. Confirmation is the rite in which we express a mature commitment to Christ, and receive strength from the Holy Spirit through prayer and the laying on of hands by a bishop.

Q. What is required of those to be confirmed?
A. It is required of those to be confirmed that they have been baptized, are sufficiently instructed in the Christian Faith, are penitent for their sins, and are ready to affirm their confession of Jesus Christ as Savior and Lord.[146]

Confirmation is the first of the Pastoral Offices in the Episcopal Book of Common Prayer. It is found after Holy Baptism and *after* The Holy Eucharist. The very structure of the book shows that confirmation has become a rite of passage for Episcopalians, and that it is not required for the baptized who wish to receive communion.

This departs from Episcopal tradition. Formerly Anglicans required confirmation before first communion.[147] But confirmation or its equivalent celebration in another communion is expected of every member:

> It is expected that all adult members of this Church, after appropriate instruction, will have made a mature public affirmation of their faith and commitment to the responsibilities of their Baptism and will have been confirmed or received by a Bishop of this Church or by a Bishop of a Church in communion with this Church.[148]

The full title of the service reads, "Confirmation with forms for Reception and for the Reaffirmation of Baptismal Vows." The Episcopal Church first established the pattern other churches have adopted: Baptism includes a rite of sealing, but the term "confirmation" is reserved for the reaffirmation of baptism, a ceremony generally for those baptized in infancy who are now coming to accept the faith and its responsibilities on their own.

The ceremony covers three circumstances. **Confirmation** is for those baptized at an early age and duly prepared "to make a mature public affirmation of their faith and commitment to the responsibilities of their Baptism and to receive the laying on of hands by the bishop."[149] Confirmation may also be celebrated by an adult immediately after baptism, if a bishop in the Episcopal church administers the sacrament. **Reception** is for those baptized in other communions, now joining the Episcopal Church. The bishop who presides confirms the new members. **Reaffirmation** is for members baptized earlier by a priest who now come to a bishop for confirmation; in the ceremony, they reaffirm their faith.

Those who wish to renew their commitment to the service of Christ in the world follow a separate order of service, "A Form of Commitment to Christian Service."[150] A bishop need not be present for this rite, which may be repeated in one's life. Confirmation with forms for Reception and Reaffirmation happens only once.

The beginning of the ritual is the same whether one was baptized as a child or has joined the church as an adult: After the word service, the candidates are presented to the bishop and renew the covenant of their baptism through the profession of their faith. Then the bishop asks a series of questions:

Will you continue in the apostles' teaching and fellowship, in the breaking of bread, and in the prayers?

Will you persevere in resisting evil, and, whenever you fall into sin, repent and return to the Lord?

Will you proclaim by word and example the Good News of God in Christ?

Will you seek and serve Christ in all persons, loving your neighbor as yourself?

Will you strive for justice and peace among all people, and respect the dignity of every human being?[151]

To each, the people reply, "I will, with God's help." Intercessions for the candidates follow, taken from the rite of Holy Baptism. The bishop then offers this prayer:

Almighty God, we thank you that by the death and resurrection of your Son Jesus Christ you have overcome sin and brought us to yourself, and that by the sealing of your Holy Spirit you have bound us to your service. Renew in *these* your *servants* the covenant you made with *them* at *their* Baptism. Send *them* forth in the power of that Spirit to perform the service you set before *them*; through Jesus Christ your Son our Lord, who lives and reigns with you and the Holy Spirit, one God, now and forever.[152]

At this point a separate prayer is offered for confirmation and for reception or reaffirmation. When confirming, the bishop lays hands upon each candidate and says,

Strengthen, O Lord, your servant N. with your Holy Spirit; empower *him*[153] for your service; and sustain *him* all the days of *his* life.

Or the bishop may say,

Defend, O Lord, your servant N. with your heavenly grace, that *he* may continue yours for ever, and daily increase in your Holy Spirit more and more, until *he* comes to your everlasting kingdom.[154]

The peace is exchanged and the eucharist may follow.

Here, the confirmation prayer asks God to strengthen the candidate with the Holy Spirit, or to increase the candidate in the Spirit more and more. The Evangelical Lutheran Church in America and the Presbyterians carefully say that this rite increases the gift of the Spirit given at baptism, so that no one might confuse the gift of the Spirit in baptism with its increase in confirmation. The Episcopal prayer, especially the first option, seems less concerned about this possible confusion.

The service of Holy Baptism in the Book of Common Prayer includes several noteworthy elements. Here alone among the churches of this chapter is found a consecration of chrism. If the bishop presides at baptism, he or she may consecrate the oil of chrism with this prayer:

> Eternal Father, whose blessed Son was anointed by the Holy Spirit to be the Savior and servant of all, we pray you to consecrate this oil, that those who are sealed with it may share in the royal priesthood of Jesus Christ; who lives and reigns with you and the Holy Spirit, for ever and ever.[155]

As in the Roman and Eastern Catholic prayers, the primary purpose for consecrating chrism is for "sealing" candidates in the priesthood of Jesus Christ. The difference is that the Episcopal Church, as shown below, seals in the baptismal rite, while the Roman and Eastern Catholic Churches seal in the confirmation rite.

After the pouring of water, the bishop or priest who presides says this prayer:

> Heavenly Father, we thank you that by water and the Holy Spirit you have bestowed upon *these* your *servants* the forgiveness of sin, and have raised *them* to the new life of grace. Sustain *them*, O Lord, in your Holy Spirit. Give *them* an inquiring and discerning heart, the courage to will and to persevere, a spirit to know and to love you, and the gift of joy and wonder in all your works.[156]

The parallel to the "confirmation" prayer in the Roman Catholic Church is clear, although the plea for the "gifts of the Spirit," adapted from Isaiah, contains more contemporary language.

After this prayer, the presider places a hand on the person's head, traces the sign of the cross (with chrism, if desired), and says,

> N. you are sealed by the Holy Spirit in Baptism and marked as Christ's own for ever.[157]

This sealing very closely resembles the sacramental sealing in confirmation or chrismation in the Roman and Eastern Catholic Churches. By inserting the phrase "in Baptism" the Episcopal Church asserts that this is not "confirmation"—confirmation has been assigned to a later ritual.

If the one to be baptized is an adult, confirmation as such may follow baptism if the bishop is present.

The Episcopal Church recognizes the confirmation received by "any Bishop in apostolic succession."[158] This includes the Roman and Eastern Churches. Thus, if a baptized and confirmed Eastern Catholic wishes to join the Anglican communion, confirmation would not take place in the service of reception.

The Methodist Church

> The term *confirmation* has three important meanings: (1) Candidates confirm their personal commitment by accepting for themselves the vows made at their baptism. (2) God reconfirms the covenant in Christ to those who were too young to understand it when they were baptized. (3) The congregation confirms these persons in their relationship to the family of Christ and in the ministries to which all Christians are commissioned by baptism.[159]

Candidates for confirmation in the Methodist Church are those who were baptized when they were too young to appreciate its meaning and responsibilities, or those baptized in other churches who now wish to join Methodism.

It is in baptism when Methodists claim God's promised "seal of the Spirit (Eph 1, 13)." But more follows.

> Baptism is followed by nurture and the consequent awareness by the baptized of the claim to ministry in Christ placed upon their lives by the Church. Such a ministry is ratified in confir-

mation, where the pledges of Baptism are accepted and renewed for life and mission.[160]

Confirmation ratifies the baptismal covenant. In confirmation a Methodist responds back to the God of baptism. Prior to confirmation, baptized Methodist children and others who seek membership in the church are called "preparatory members." Only in confirmation are they duly enrolled as full members of the United Methodist Church.[161]

The baptismal covenant for Methodists may be celebrated according to four different services. The first is a new, single service offering "Holy Baptism, Confirmation, Reaffirmation of Faith, Reception into the United Methodist Church, and Reception into a Local Congregation." The second is for "Holy Baptism for Children and Others Unable to Answer for Themselves," which does not, of course, include confirmation. The third covers the same circumstances as the first, but offers the traditional text from the former Methodist and former Evangelical United Brethren churches. And the fourth is a "Congregational Reaffirmation of the Baptismal Covenant," which, like the second, does not include a service for confirmation.

Candidates for confirmation are those baptized "before they are old enough to take the vows for themselves." However, "those who are able to take the vows for themselves at their baptism are not confirmed, for they have made their public profession of faith at the font."[162] That means that Methodists who are baptized as adults are not confirmed.

The confirmation ritual is quite simple: After the candidates confess their faith, water may be blessed if it is to be used for the reaffirmation of faith. "Water may be used symbolically in ways that cannot be interpreted as baptism, as the pastor says, 'Remember your baptism and be thankful.' "[163]

Then the pastor places hands on the head of each one being confirmed; others may join him. The pastor says,

> *Name*, the Holy Spirit work within you, that having been born through water and the Spirit, you may live as a faithful disciple of Jesus Christ.[164]

Other rites of reception may follow. Afterward, the pastor adds for all who have been baptized, confirmed, or received,

> The God of all grace, who has called us to eternal glory in Christ, establish you and strengthen you by the power of the Holy Spirit, that you may live in grace and peace.[165]

Thus, for the Methodists confirmation prays that the Holy Spirit may be at work within the baptized to help them live discipleship faithfully. It is accompanied by the imposition of hands. The ritual is exactly the same for those who wish to reaffirm their baptism at any other time in life. The term "confirmation" refers to the first time this reaffirmation takes place, for those baptized when they were young.

The baptismal ritual is almost the same. After the pouring of the water, the pastor places hands on the head of each candidate. Others may join in the gesture. The pastor says to each,

> The Holy Spirit work within you, that being born through water and the Spirit, you may be a faithful disciple of Jesus Christ.[166]

This text differs from confirmation only in the tense of a participle: In baptism, the newly baptized is "being born through water and the Spirit," and in confirmation the candidate is one "having been born through water and the Spirit." Methodism carefully acknowledges that the activity of the Spirit begins in baptism, and is continued in confirmation. The use of oil is nowhere recommended.

The third form of the baptismal covenant also includes a service of confirmation. The text reads as follows:

> Name, the Lord defend you with his heavenly grace and by his Spirit confirm you in the faith and fellowship of all true disciples of Jesus Christ.[167]

Again, the ritual is quite simple. One's full participation in the community of believers is implied by this text.

The baptismal ritual includes a prayer for the coming of the

Holy Spirit, and an optional tracing of the cross. These elements imitate the original location of confirmation in the sacraments of initiation, between the pouring of water and the first reception of the eucharist.

But for the Methodists confirmation has taken its place as a rite of personal acceptance of faith and full membership in the church, celebrated many years after baptism.

Themes

All the churches considered in this chapter have placed confirmation squarely among the rites of reaffirming baptism. They see it as one of several ways Christians reaffirm their baptismal covenant. The Presbyterians do not use the word "confirmation," but the parallels are evident. All but the Methodists permit the use of oil. And all include elements of the patristic origins of confirmation in their baptismal rites.

That they choose to assign the name "confirmation" to the rite of professing one's own faith (rather than to the sealing in baptism) shows the influence of the great leaders of the Reform (notably Luther and John Calvin), the late medieval tradition out of which they worked, and the enduring tradition of several hundred intervening years.

Concerns

In grouping these churches together under one heading it is wise not to succumb to the temptation of treating them as a single unit, or to expect commonality with their practices. There are many common elements in the way Protestant-Anglican churches approach confirmation, but there are differences as well. And as in any model of confirmation, there are concerns.

The Gift of the Spirit

As already noted, these churches exhibit concern over the unspoken question, "How could the Holy Spirit come in confirmation if the same Spirit has already come in baptism?"

When the Reformers criticized Catholic confirmation, they said that making confirmation a sacrament of the gift of the Holy Spirit implies that baptism does not include the gift of the Spirit. The Catholic Church never maintained that position, but the confusion is understandable.

Protestant-Anglican churches handle the matter in different ways, but the question they raise concerns all who celebrate baptism and some further ritual of the Spirit. The gift of the Holy Spirit in baptism should not be compromised.

Sacramentality

Although the Catholic Church continues to maintain that the sacraments number seven, those of the Reform still recognize only two, baptism and the eucharist. The inability of all Christian churches to resolve the matter remains an obstacle to the restoration of full communion. Confirmation is but one pawn in the game. Still, in arguing the meaning of confirmation, churches will reach consensus only when they agree on the nature of sacraments themselves.

"Confirmation"

Almost universally, Protestant-Anglican churches assign the name "confirmation" to the affirmation of the baptism one received at an earlier age. Yet, again almost universally, they include a rite of "sealing" in the baptismal service. Is "confirmation" the right rite?

Historically, the term did not come into prominence until after the bishop's anointing had split away from the baptismal rite of initiation, but the term continues to be used for many different circumstances in Christianity as a whole.

Further, the origins of the word seem to come from an action of the bishop: The bishop "confirmed" the baptism at which a presbyter had presided. Frequently the services examined above expand on the meaning of the word: God confirms the candidates, the people confirm their membership, the candidates confirm their faith. All this sounds quite poetic, but it adds to the confusion of just who is confirming what and why this rite carries the name it does.

Eligibility

Who the candidates are for confirmation may differ from one church to another. The question is especially apparent when one member transfers into one of these churches from another denomination. The Episcopalians confirm new members coming from certain other churches, but not from all. The Methodists do not confirm those baptized as adults, even in their own faith. The Evangelical Lutheran Church in America confirms the baptized, but those transferring affiliations celebrate reception into membership or restoration to membership. Again, one should not expect uniformity among all these churches, but the differences in eligibility further obscure the meaning of confirmation.

Membership

The Evangelical Lutheran Church in America has carefully eliminated the concept of membership from confirmation. They believe that all the baptized are fully members of the church, fully eligible for communion. The Lutheran Church—Missouri Synod keeps the language of "membership" in the confirmation rite.

The Methodists accept the baptized as "preparatory members," and see confirmation as one's admission to the status of "full membership." For them, baptism in a sense confers an incomplete membership until the matured Christian makes a personal response. For Presbyterians a personal profession of faith qualifies a member for full participation in the church.

These differences raise the important question about the efficacy of a child's baptism. Is personal faith required? Does the faith of the community suffice? All would agree that infant baptism absolutely confers God's grace, but they differ over its implications for church membership.

Sequence

In revising the rites of baptism and its affirmation, all these churches have placed confirmation out of the traditional sequence of baptism-confirmation-eucharist. The original sequence is maintained only if one accepts the sealing in the baptismal rite as the successor to the patristic origins of confirmation. What's unclear, then, is whether the original sequence has been disturbed at all, or if the terms are just too entangled to tell the difference.

Oil

The optional use of oil in several of these churches is a welcome addition. It opens the door to great liturgical traditions. Only the Episcopal Church specifies that the oil should be consecrated by a bishop, and it alone provides a text for the prayer. The development of the use of oil in these churches could help in ecumenical progress. Still, in current practice, it's clear that in the Catholic Church, the use of oil dominates the imposition of hands, and in Protestant-Anglican churches, the imposition of hands dominates over the use of oil.

The Minister

Who administers confirmation also differs among the churches. The Episcopal Church clearly assigns this service to the bishop; others make it the province of the pastor. Eastern Rites have always permitted the baptizing priest to chrismate as well. The Roman Catholic Church has recently expanded the occasions on which a priest may confirm. In short, there is no universal practice, or clear direction.

Practice

One other practical point should be made. One should not confuse the printed ritual texts with actual pastoral practice. Just because the Presbyterian Church, for example, has a new trial form of baptism does not mean that Presbyterian pastors now anoint the newly baptized. This chapter has examined the similarities and differences in ritual texts; they are many. But the differences in pastoral practice are even more. What the ritual book of any church says is not what actually happens in the sanctuary. The books should help toward a more uniform celebration of confirmation, but the accomplishment of that goal may be generations away.

4

Catholic Initiation

Introduction

This chapter concerns the Catholic confirmation of "candidates." This term has a specific meaning in the order of Christian initiation of adults. This chapter will not consider those baptized Catholic as infants who, through normal catechesis, later become "candidates" for confirmation. Rather, "candidates" in this chapter will refer to the following groups: 1) those baptized in other churches who are now joining the Catholic Church, 2) those baptized as Catholics but who received no catechesis for confirmation or first eucharist, and 3) those baptized as Catholics who after baptism adhered to a non-Catholic religion.[168]

When a candidate joins full communion, a simple ritual is followed:[169] The celebrant invites the candidates and sponsors forward. The candidates recite the Nicene Creed or (if the ritual takes place at the Easter Vigil) renew their baptismal promises. The candidates then add this sentence:

I believe and profess all that the holy Catholic Church believes, teaches, and proclaims to be revealed by God.[170]

Then the celebrant proclaims the Act of Reception to each,

N., the Lord receives you into the Catholic Church. His loving kindness has led you here, so that in the unity of the Holy Spirit you may have full communion with us in the faith that you have professed in the presence of his family.[171]

Confirmation follows.

There is one exception. If the candidate comes from a church in schism (more on this distinction later), and if the candidate has been confirmed or chrismated, confirmation is omitted. This includes any Orthodox Church, the Old Catholic Church, the Polish Catholic Church, and the Society of St. Pius X. When confirmation is omitted, the presider lays his right hand on the candidate while he proclaims the Act of Reception.

Thus, confirmation shares the rites of "Catholic initiation": It follows the profession of faith for candidates who were baptized years earlier. This contrasts with "Christian initiation" when confirmation immediately follows the baptism of catechumens.

The rite of confirmation is identical in both cases. In fact, at the Easter Vigil Catholics frequently witness first the baptism of catechumens, then the profession of faith of the candidates, and the confirmation of both groups together. Although the rite of confirmation is the same for both circumstances, this chapter will show how its meaning differs.

Children of catechetical age follow the same pattern as adults. The order of Christian initiation of adults is confusing on this point: It provides rituals for unbaptized children who have reached catechetical age,[172] and for the preparation of baptized, uncatechized adults for confirmation and eucharist.[173] It does not so precisely address the question of which rituals to celebrate for baptized, uncatechized children. However, the code of canon law grants a presbyter (priest) the faculty to confirm anyone "already baptized whom he admits into the full communion of the Catholic Church."[174] And it says "a presbyter who has this faculty must use it for those in whose favor the faculty was granted."[175] So, for example, if baptized Lutheran children join the Catholic Church with their parents, the priest who confirms the parents confirms the children as well.

In this case, confirmation parallels a rite of "reception" or transfer of membership in a Protestant-Anglican church: Confirmation prays for the gift of the Holy Spirit upon those now professing faith in a new body of believers.

Confirmation: the same name and the same ritual are used both for the newly baptized and for those professing faith in the

Catholic Church. But the confirmation of those already baptized carries extra meanings.

This chapter will explain the additional meanings confirmation carries in Catholic initiation. It will then return to a historical survey to find precedents for this interpretation. Finally it will compare the rites for transferring membership among the churches studied in earlier chapters.

Meanings

Confirmation retains its primary meanings: It celebrates the gift of the Holy Spirit and conforms the new member to be more like Christ. However, other interpretations may be added.

Catholic unity: This gift of the Holy Spirit celebrates the unity the new member has with other Catholics. This unity prepares the one confirmed to receive the eucharist, the great sacrament of unity. Vatican II says those are fully incorporated into the community of the church who "possessing the Spirit of Christ accept the church's whole organization and all the means of salvation founded in it."[176] This could allude to confirmation: Full incorporation into the church includes the sacramental celebration of the gifts of the Holy Spirit.[177] Confirmation could be called part of the rites of membership in the church. After the candidates profess their faith, the community responds with the sacrament of the Spirit who unifies the members of the church.

Reconciliation: It seems that the imposition of hands implies reconciliation as well as the coming of the Spirit. In confirming a candidate baptized in another denomination, the church assumes that Catholic membership reconciles part of the broken Christian community. Liturgically the new member does not approach as a penitent, but confirmation retains a disciplinary air, which originated more explicitly in the early church.

The Reconciliation of Heretics

In the early days of the church, some Christians drifted to heresy or schism, and others were baptized by heretics. Occasionally, these who were outside the church asked to be reconciled with orthodox Christianity.[178] The faithful then had to decide whether and how to bring them back into the fold.

Orthodox Christianity distinguished between schismatics and heretics.[179] Schismatics dissented from certain points of Christian belief and practice; but heretics committed serious doctrinal error.

Customs varied from age to age and region to region, but generally speaking the reconciliation took place either through the imposition of hands or an anointing with chrism. Exceptions exist, but a trend gradually developed whereby schismatics were reconciled by the imposition of hands and heretics by an anointing with chrism.[180]

The two symbols carried different meanings. The imposition of hands for schismatics served not only as a symbol for the Holy Spirit, but as a sign of reconciliation. This was true even in baptism, where one effect of the waters is to cleanse from sin. Anointing served as a stronger symbol for heretics. Lifted from the orthodox baptismal ceremony it "completed" the baptism of the heretics. More than reconciliatory, this rite may have arisen from fears that the heretical baptism needed completion, since the effects of baptism had not been evident.

Thus in the early centuries, even before confirmation split from baptism, the church took baptismal symbols (the imposition of hands and/or anointing), separated them from baptism, and applied them to the reconciliation of heretics.[181]

By borrowing the same baptismal elements which developed into confirmation, the church introduced another development of confirmation in the practice of reconciling heretics. This early practice seems to be the ancestor for the custom of confirming those who join the Catholic Church from another Christian church. It is no longer called reconciling, but the parallels are evident.

Now a distinction can be made between two aspects of confirmation that are joined today: the gift of the Spirit and sealing with the Spirit. In the case of reconciling heretics, the anointing with chrism stressed more clearly the theme of "sealing." Those who were baptized had already received the Holy Spirit; now in their coming to orthodox Christianity, they were "sealed" in this reconciliation. The faithful who received the imposition of hands and anointing as part of the normal orthodox baptismal liturgy, however, more clearly received the "gift" of the Holy Spirit, for here the Spirit was coming for the first time in all the rites accompanying the water bath of baptism.[182] Today, the themes of gift and sealing are spoken of together, no matter what the occasion for confirmation. But a case can be made for the influence of reconciliation in their early development.[183]

Who Confirms New Members

Not all churches confirm their new members. A summary follows for several church groups:

The Roman Catholic Church: The Catholic Church distinguishes two admission practices—one for those joining from Orthodox Christianity (and other churches in schism), the other from Protestant-Anglican churches (and others seriously separated).

When a Roman Catholic community welcomes into communion a candidate from Orthodoxy, that candidate canonically joins an Eastern Catholic Rite, not the Roman Catholic Rite. This will be explained in more detail below.

The Roman Catholic Church takes a different approach with those coming from the Protestant-Anglican churches. In all cases, even when those received into the Catholic Church have been confirmed in another church, new members celebrate the sacrament of confirmation.

Principally, there are two reasons why this is done. The first is that Protestant-Anglican churches do not regard confirmation as a sacrament.[184] Generally, they accept two sacraments, baptism and the Lord's Supper, but following the original work of Luther, they class confirmation in a different category of rituals. This means they differ from Catholics in their understanding of the role confirmation plays for the community. Catholics believe confirmation is a sacramental encounter with the risen Christ on the same order as baptism and eucharist; other churches do not believe it carries that force.

The second reason Catholics celebrate confirmation with

those joining from Protestant-Anglican churches is that the Catholic Church has never formally recognized apostolic succession in those churches, nor therefore the ordination of their clergy. Since the administration of confirmation is reserved in the Catholic Church to bishops and priests, Catholics do not recognize the validity of confirmation in another church even if it does call it a sacrament. The non-recognition of orders remains a painful point in the ecumenical dialogue.

Sometimes baptized candidates for communion in the Catholic Church ask why they must be "confirmed again" before receiving communion. The above reasons may be given—Protestants do not regard their confirmation as a sacrament; the Catholic Church does not accept others' ordinations—but it is also true that the purpose of confirmation for the two groups is not the same. The Protestant-Anglican churches generally see confirmation as a kind of "coming of age" ritual, a maturity rite for Christians marking an advance in catechesis. Traditionally, Catholics have understood confirmation as the gift of the Holy Spirit: a rite of initiation or of strengthening. Especially for the Eastern Rites there is little relationship between the chrismation of an infant and the catechized maturing of a young Protestant's faith. Yet both stand under the umbrella of Christian usages for the term "confirmation." Another reason for celebrating confirmation at the time of reception is that it has ritualized unity with and reconciliation in the Catholic Church.

Those confirmed in other churches might more properly ask why they must be confirmed in the Catholic Church if they have been *baptized,* since Christian baptism in any denomination generally includes the basic meaning of confirmation in Catholicism: the gift of the Holy Spirit. The reason is that Catholic confirmation of those baptized in other faiths carries additional meanings: sacramentality, unity, and reconciliation, and these prepare the new member for Catholic communion.

The Eastern Catholic Churches: As recorded in chapter 2, Eastern Catholic Churches defer chrismation from baptism only on two occasions, both involving the reception of new members. If the new members come from the Roman Catholic Church before they were confirmed, or from one of the Protestant-Anglican churches, the Eastern Church chrismates them.

The Catholic Church does not confirm those coming from Eastern Orthodox Rites, even though they are not in union with Rome.[185] The reason is that the Catholic Church accepts all the sacraments of the Eastern Orthodox Rites, as it does for any church in schism. Catholics believe that schismatic churches share with them the same apostolic succession—the faithful handing down of the sacraments since the time of Christ. In Orthodoxy that succession grants all Rites the priesthood and the eucharist.[186] Despite overtures to reconciliation between east and west, the two major groups remain apart.

For this reason, when Orthodox Christians join the Catholic Church they make a profession of faith and receive communion, but they are not confirmed, since Catholics regard chrismation—even Orthodox chrismation—the same as the sacrament of confirmation.[187] However, when the celebrant proclaims the Act of Reception for an Orthodox candidate, he lays a hand on his or her head. (This same procedure applies to all received into the Catholic Church from churches in schism, including the Old Catholic Church, the Polish Catholic Church, and the Society of St. Pius X.)

In the case of Orthodoxy, the new Catholics join not the Roman Catholic Church, but the Catholic Rite of their Orthodox family.[188] So, a Russian Orthodox who aspires to full Catholic communion joins the Russian Catholic Church, even though the profession of faith may be made before a Roman Catholic community. Since the Catholic Churches all share communion, a Russian Catholic enjoys all the sacramental privileges of a Roman Catholic. What's different is the Rite of membership and the bishop. If the new Eastern Catholic wishes to join the *Roman* Catholic Church, he or she would apply to the Apostolic Nunciature through the local bishop for the process of transfer,[189] but the Roman Catholic community must take care not to force such a transfer.[190] Such care will help preserve the rich traditions of all Catholic Rites.

The laws for children parallel those for adults. Among Eastern Catholics, children under the age of fourteen are baptized into the Rite of their father. But if only the mother is Catholic or if both parents agree, children may join the mother's Rite.[191] After age fourteen, unbaptized children may choose which Rite they wish to join.[192] If, after baptism in a Catholic Rite, a child wishes to transfer to another Catholic Rite, he or she may do so after age fourteen through the regular process. This does not include chrismation since the child was chrismated at baptism. An Orthodox child joining Catholic communion joins the Catholic Rite of the same family, as noted above for adults. That child does not celebrate confirmation, since his or her baptism included chrismation.

Orthodox Churches: As a general rule, churches of the Orthodox Rites chrismate all new members, since they recognize no other church's sacraments, except baptism. The Greek Orthodox Church and those related to Constantinople chrismate confirmed Catholics joining their Rite.[193] The Russian Orthodox accept Catholic members by a profession of faith. Surprisingly, all in the Orthodox family may also *re-chrismate* their own members in the case where someone chooses a non-Christian religion for a time and then wishes to be restored to membership in Orthodoxy.[194] Such cases are extremely rare.[195] Although the church believes that "chrismation, once canonically performed, cannot be repeated," it believes that "chrismation is also a sacrament of reconciliation."[196] Thus, if chrismation is repeated, it carries the specific theme of reconciliation.[197]

Protestant-Anglican Churches: As noted above, Protestant-Anglican churches do not all require confirmation for new members. Methodists and the Evangelical Lutheran Church in America reserve confirmation for those baptized in their own denomination; affirmation of baptism takes another form for those joining from another church. The Episcopal Church confirms Protestants but not Catholics. Presbyterians do not use the term "confirmation." Missouri Synod Lutherans confirm all new members.

To summarize, in the Catholic Church, candidates celebrate confirmation with their profession of faith. The primary purpose of this celebration is to accent the seal of the Spirit on the new members and their unity with other Catholics. In the Eastern Rites, chrismation follows the same purpose. In Orthodoxy, chrismating new members shows their unity with the Orthodox faith, and chrismation is required of all new members. In rare instances, an Orthodox Christian may receive chrismation twice. Among Protestant churches, confirmation is frequently not administered for those joining the church. Rather, that occasion is marked by another ceremony, the affirmation of baptism. New Anglicans are confirmed unless they come from one of the Catholic or Orthodox Churches.

Concerns

Concerns arise over new meanings of confirmation in this context: denominational membership and reconciliation.

Analyzing confirmation as the rite for baptized Christians to transfer their membership from one church to another reveals additional meanings to the sacrament. Not just a sacrament of Christian initiation, not just a sacrament of maturity, confirmation has become a sacrament of membership in a particular Christian church. Taken to its extreme this looks like baptism makes one a Christian, but confirmation makes one a Catholic, an Episcopalian, or an Orthodox Christian. This could never have been the purpose for confirmation in its origins: not as the fifth century rite where the bishop "confirmed" the action of the baptizing presbyter, not as the third century imposition of hands and/or anointing which underscored the gift of the Spirit in the rites of initiation, and certainly not as the apostolic gesture to mark the coming of the Holy Spirit on those professing faith in Christ. Seen in its complexity here, as a ceremony several churches use for membership, it ritualizes division more than unity.[198]

Although confirmation continues to be celebrated among Catholic, Orthodox, Missouri Synod Lutheran, and Anglican churches on the occasion of welcoming a new member who is already baptized, other churches no longer use the term for those occasions. Perhaps they wish to honor the confirmation of sister churches; perhaps they wish to honor the coming of the Holy Spirit in baptism. Perhaps they think confirmation is a bad idea, so they let new members "slip in" like refugees who ran around the Berlin Wall in the late 1980's before it finally fell, hoping this confusion would simply go away. In any case, they imply that the prayer for the Spirit traditionally called "confirmation" is not necessary for membership. Should the Catholics, Orthodox, Missouri Synod Lutherans, and Anglicans retain their insistence that confirmation/chrismation is something unique? Or will they gradually welcome new members without it, tacitly accepting the gift of the Spirit in other churches' baptism? A solution will require agreeing on the meaning of confirmation, the nature of a sacrament, and the acceptance of orders.

Another concern is the theme of reconciliation. Celebrated as a rite of membership in these churches, confirmation becomes a means of reconciliation for something broken in the body of Christ. At the time of the Reformation, Catholics regarded Protestants as heretics, and Protestants thought the same of Catholics. Today the churches rarely label each other in this way, preferring to accent the Christian beliefs they hold in common, but the inability to share eucharist from a common table demonstrates that they still imply the accusation.

Antagonism between these churches is implied in the way Catholics initiate new members. When they receive an Orthodox Christian into the church, they do not confirm the new member, but the celebrant does lay a hand on him or her. This gesture recalls the imposition of the hand used in the early days of the church to reconcile those returning from schism. When Catholics receive Protestants into the church, they confirm the new member with an anointing. This gesture recalls the patristic era anointing which reconciled those returning from heresy.

Confirmation thus becomes a rite of reconciliation, in which new members are sealed with the gift of the Holy Spirit. Although this ritual has ancient roots, it raises questions: How long will the ecumenical movement continue to tolerate the implication that Protestants and/or Catholics are heretics? If reconciliation is appropriate, why celebrate confirmation?

A familiar question returns: Just what does confirmation mean? If confirmation is the gift of the Spirit, does that not occur in baptism—any Christian baptism? If confirmation is a strengthening of the baptismal gift of the Holy Spirit, must it accompany the reception of new members?[199] Should it? Would a rite of reconciliation be more fitting? If so, why confirm? If confirmation signifies membership or reconciliation, has it not derived yet another meaning to add to the confusion already surrounding the occasion and age for its celebration?

Equally confusing is the practice in the Eastern Rites, Catholic and Orthodox, which presents new occasions for chrismation.

Eastern Catholics chrismate unconfirmed Roman Catholics and those joining from Protestant-Anglican churches. Chrismation, no longer the exclusive territory of baptismal initiation, marks a transfer of membership. The Orthodox take this to the extreme of *repeating* chrismation for new members from Catholic churches[200] *and* for returning members having drifted to non-Christian faiths for a time.[201] If chrismation highlights the baptismal seal of initiation, is it necessary for those whose baptism is long past? If it is repeatable does it really carry the lasting presence of the Holy Spirit? Is chrismation really the same as confirmation?

These different practices mean confirmation will be interpreted in many different ways. One term carries the burden of many meanings.

5

Confirmation of Children

Introduction

The Catholic Church publishes a rite of confirmation for those baptized in infancy whose confirmation was deferred. The ritual is very similar to the one in adult initiation, but the occasion is different: The *Rite of Confirmation* is an independent ritual; in adult initiation baptism immediately precedes it. This separate occasion offers its own nuance to the meaning of the sacrament.

This chapter will summarize the three documents which make up the published rite, and then explain several themes which recur throughout them all.

The Published Texts

The three documents in question are the Decree of the Sacred Congregation for Divine Worship, the Apostolic Constitution on the Sacrament of Confirmation, and the rite or order of confirmation with its ritual texts and explanations.

The Decree

The purpose of the Decree was to announce that the new ritual of confirmation is now available. Vatican II's Constitution on the Sacred Liturgy called for this revision in 1963.[202] The Decree, a brief letter from the Vatican Congregation responsible for the revision, announced its completion in 1971.

The Decree comprises three parts: First, it describes the purpose and origins of confirmation—the gift of the Holy Spirit strengthening one to give witness, originating with the apostles. Then, it recalls the purpose of the revision—to make clearer the connection of confirmation with Christian initiation. Finally, it proclaims that the revision is completed.[203]

The Apostolic Constitution

The lengthier theological treatise that introduces the ritual is signed by Pope Paul VI.[204]

First, he places confirmation in its context with initiation. He says the revised rite complies with the "pastoral purpose" of Vatican II. Mainly, though, he intends to describe what concerns the essence of the rite, through which the faithful receive the Holy Spirit.

Paul then situates confirmation against the New Testament accounts of the Holy Spirit—how the Spirit came to Jesus, impelled him forth, and assisted him in his work. He recalls the same Spirit came to the apostles, and states that the sacrament today celebrates a similar sharing of the Spirit.

Paul then traces the history of confirmation in east and west. True to his purpose to describe what concerns the essence of the rite, he describes the central actions and words throughout this history. Among actions, he observes the importance of anointing in both east and west, even though the imposition of hands was never lost.

With regard to the use of words in the rite, Paul notes that the apostles prayed when they imposed hands on new believers. The east and west, however, differed in the words for the rite. Eastern priests said, "The seal of the gift of the Holy Spirit," and western bishops said, "I sign you with the sign of the cross and confirm you with the chrism of salvation. In the name of the Father and of the Son and of the Holy Spirit."

Paul concludes his treatise by describing what will be the essence—the words and the actions—for the revised rite: He boldly changed a long-standing tradition in the west, and adopted the words of the Byzantine Rite with a minor adaptation (literally, "*N., receive* the seal of the gift of the Holy Spirit"). The essential action, he specified, would remain the anointing, but the imposition of hands should be held in high esteem.

The Order of Confirmation

The order of confirmation follows, beginning with its introduction. Five parts make up the introduction: the meaning, the ministers, the celebration, the adaptations, and the preparations of confirmation.

The first part explains that confirmation is part of initiation, that the gift of the Holy Spirit conforms believers more perfectly to Christ and strengthens them to bear witness.

Second, the introduction explains the various ministries involved in confirmation: The people and pastors alike prepare those to be confirmed. In the case of child candidates, their parents should participate in sacraments. The whole people of God should share in a festive and solemn liturgy. Sponsors present the candidates and help them throughout their lives. The bishop is the original minister of the sacrament, though he may share this duty with priests.

Next the introduction describes the celebration of confirmation. It discusses the "essential" elements: the words ("Be sealed with the Gift of the Holy Spirit"), the oil (chrism, blessed by a bishop), and the importance of the imposition of hands. It considers special circumstances: catechumens, and adults and adolescents who were baptized as infants. It describes eligibility and catechesis for the sacrament. It suggests that confirmation be celebrated at Mass, and urges the pastor to make proper records.

The fourth section guides adaptations for the rite, and the fifth notes what materials are needed to prepare for the liturgy (e.g., vestments, chairs, books, etc.).

Following this introduction the order of confirmation is then divided into five chapters: Rite of Confirmation Within Mass, Rite of Confirmation Outside Mass, Rite of Confirmation by a Minister Who Is Not a Bishop, Confirmation of a Person in Danger of Death, and Texts for the Celebration of Confirmation.

These titles explain themselves. Each section of the rite includes both texts and commentary to help those celebrating understand the flow and meaning of the rite.

It may surprise that the order of confirmation includes a

chapter describing its celebration outside Mass. The order suggests that this adaptation pertains to children who have not yet received first eucharist and will not at this liturgy.[205] Originally, however, the compilers of the liturgy worried about the length of the service. Vatican II cautiously allowed that "Confirmation may be conferred within Mass when convenient," but asked for an order of service outside of Mass to be written.[206] Even the code of canon law permits a bishop to enjoy the help of priests in administering the sacrament "for a grave cause."[207] Indeed, the grave cause seems to have been the length of the service! Bernard Botte says the expanded permissions for priests to confirm allowed confirmation to change from a ritual action celebrated often without Scripture readings to one which could include the Mass.[208] Thus, the order of confirmation outside Mass responded to the initial fears about the length of a ceremony at which the bishop alone ministered to large numbers of candidates.

Themes

Throughout these many texts several themes recur which shed light on the meaning of confirmation according to this model. What age is being considered? This model concerns an occasion for confirmation (i.e., deferred from baptism) more than a particular age. Because the movement toward adolescent confirmation contains its own thematic structure and design, originating from catechesis rather than from liturgy, it will be analyzed in the next chapter of this book, so this chapter will discuss the meaning of delayed confirmation for pre-adolescents. The order of confirmation pertains to a fairly broad spectrum of ages, which find unity in the occasion of the sacrament rather than in the age of the one being confirmed.

Recurrent themes include the following: initiation, strengthening, likeness to Christ, witness, the gift of the Holy Spirit, the church, and the origins of the sacrament.

Initiation

Initiation surfaces as the most important theme. Vatican II asked for the rite of confirmation to be revised precisely because of this theme: that it is a sacrament of initiation.[209] The Decree admits this is the whole purpose of the revision. Since the order of baptism for children was already in use, the order of confirmation was published "to show the unity of Christian initiation in its true light."[210] The ritual begins by acknowledging that "those who have been baptized continue on the path of Christian initiation through the sacrament of confirmation."[211]

Several texts demonstrate how the liturgy seeks to make the sacrament available to the baptized. For example, priests are given faculties to confirm under certain circumstances,[212] multiplying the number of ministers available. When the sacrament is postponed beyond the seventh year, "precautions should be taken so that children will . . . not be deprived of the benefit of this sacrament."[213] Further, if confirmation preparation shares time with marriage preparation, it may be better to defer confirmation after marriage for a "fruitful reception" of the sacrament.[214] This indicates the seriousness with which the liturgy takes confirmation. Finally, those in danger of death should be given the sacrament with whatever spiritual preparation is possible.[215] Thus, the liturgy regards confirmation as an important part of initiation, worthy of preparation, but to be made readily available to those for whom it was deferred.

Confirmation's connection with the other sacraments of initiation is shown forth "not only by closer association of these sacraments but also by the rite and words."[216] This "closer association" could concern the sequence or the lapsed time in celebrating the sacraments of initiation.[217] The rite and words will also show confirmation's connection to baptism. Several examples follow.

Those to be confirmed must meet certain requirements. They must have been baptized, be in a state of grace, and able to renew their baptismal promises.[218] Their preparation may follow regionally authorized catechetical guidelines.[219] Adults baptized as infants who have not yet been confirmed should follow a preparation adapted from the catechumenate.[220] Thus, the preparation for confirmation mimics the preparation for adult baptismal initiation. The Decree even states that initiation is "completed" with confirmation.

Another comparison to baptism arises in the role of the confirmation sponsor. Just as the newly baptized are accompanied by a godparent who introduces them to the Christian life and helps them grow in it after baptism, so those to be confirmed enjoy the companionship of a sponsor for similar reasons.[221] It is preferable that the confirmation sponsor be the baptismal godparent.[222] Sponsors should be mature, fully initiated members of the Catholic Church not prohibited by law from exercising the role; if parents present the candidate, they are not "sponsors" in the strictest sense.[223] The sponsor's role is to present the candidate (sometimes by name),[224] and to place his or her right hand on the candidate's shoulder.[225] This role shows the community presenting and supporting one of its own.

The imposition of hands[226] figures into the initiatory imagery. Although it does not recall the baptismal rite, it does recall the gesture used by the apostles when—the liturgy says—they were "completing baptism."[227]

Finally, the initiatory symbolism reaches its climax in the relationship between confirmation and eucharist, especially first eucharist. Adults baptized in infancy should "receive confirmation and the eucharist in a common celebration."[228] "Ordinarily confirmation takes place within Mass in order to express more clearly the fundamental connection of this sacrament with the entirety of Christian initiation."[229] However, if children who have not received the eucharist are not admitted to first communion on this occasion, "confirmation should be celebrated outside Mass."[230]

Clearly this anomaly should be avoided. The liturgy of the eucharist normally follows,[231] and communion should be given under both forms.[232] The rite of confirmation concludes with a sign of peace.[233] This liturgical gesture most frequently indicates one's readiness for eucharist.[234] Catechumens are dismissed from the liturgy before the kiss of peace, and only after their baptism do they share peace with the full Christian assembly in preparation for eucharist. The inclusion of the sign of peace in the rite of confirmation indicates the readiness of the newly confirmed to receive the eucharist.

Absent from the ritual is the former practice of taking an additional name. This custom originated from imitating the baptismal ritual, and signified a new direction in the life of the Christian. The omission of the new name argues for the importance of the baptismal name throughout one's life, and against the belief that confirmation begins a new decisive moment in the life of the Christian.

The theme of initiation may explain why one effect of confirmation is to bind the Christian more closely to the Church.[235]

Strengthening

Another theme which stands out from the liturgy is strengthening. Strengthening results from confirmation.

Christian initiation follows "the origin, development, and nourishing of natural life."[236] Confirmation conforms to "development" in the Christian life. Through the three sacraments of initiation the faithful "receive in increasing measure the treasures of divine life and advance toward the perfection of charity."[237] Thus confirmation is an increase, a strengthening, a new degree of Christian life. The Constitution quotes one of the earliest of the Church Fathers, Tertullian, who interprets some of the symbols of initiation: "The body is anointed, that the soul may be consecrated; the body is signed, that the soul too may be fortified."[238] This theme is echoed in one of the optional opening prayers for confirmation, which asks that the Holy Spirit will help the candidates "grow in the strength of his love to the full stature of Christ."[239]

Both the Decree and the Apostolic Constitution allude to this strengthening, and the Constitution quotes Vatican II on this point: those confirmed "are endowed with the special strength of the Holy Spirit."[240] The liturgy specifically prays for this strength just before the imposition of hands: "Let us pray to the Father that he will pour out the Holy Spirit to strengthen his sons and daughters with his gifts."[241]

Those familiar with the old order of confirmation will note the absence of its most infamous gesture: the bishop's slap to the cheek of the newly confirmed. The slap, given "lightly" according to the rubrics, suited the theme of strengthening. It symbolized the Christian's soldier-like ability to withstand adversity to the faith.[242] Its omission admits the gesture was frequently misinterpreted. Ironically, it's likely that the slap evolved from the sign of peace.

More Like Christ

The nature of this strengthening makes one more like Christ. "The giving of the Holy Spirit conforms believers more perfectly to Christ."[243] The relationship to Christ is ritualized in the anointing. "Christ" means "anointed one," and the term derives from "chrism." To anoint with chrism is to make one "Christ." Thus, the prayer during the imposition of hands asks the Holy Spirit to "anoint (the candidates) to be more like Christ the Son of God."[244] Chrism is applied in the sign of Christ's cross.[245]

This likeness to Christ results from the "character" confirmation imparts. One of the three sacraments given only once, confirmation is said to impart a "character" indicating its irrepeatability. This character, "the seal of the Lord," conforms the confirmed "more closely to Christ."[246] The suggested homily says, "The gift of the Holy Spirit which you are to receive will be a spiritual sign and seal to make you more like Christ and more perfect members of his Church."[247] Thus the liturgy links the irrepeatable nature of confirmation with this result of the sacrament—that it makes one more like Christ.

This theme is echoed in the prayers over the gifts for the liturgy: "Send us your Spirit to make us more like Christ in bearing witness to the world,"[248] and "Lord, you have signed our brothers and sisters with the cross of your Son and anointed them with the oil of salvation. As they offer themselves with Christ, continue to fill their hearts with your Spirit."[249]

The final blessing asks Christ to bless the newly confirmed and give them "courage in professing the true faith."[250] Conformity to Christ thus introduces the theme of witness.

Witness

Giving witness was the work of Christ to whom those being confirmed are conformed. Jesus began his mission after the Spirit came upon him at his baptism in the Jordan. The same Spirit impelled the apostles into ministry at Pentecost and urges the same result for all Christians in confirmation.

In confirmation Christians are "made true witnesses of Christ in word and deed."[251] The Holy Spirit strengthens them "so that they may bear witness to Christ for the building up of his body in faith and love."[252] The bishop's ministry evolved from that of the apostles. His presence at confirmation shows the very work of apostles, "the mandate to be witnesses of Christ."[253] Chrism, in conforming one to Christ, gives "the grace of spreading the Lord's presence."[254]

Several liturgical texts pick up the same theme. The suggested homily admonishes the candidates, "You must be witnesses before all the world to (Christ's) suffering, death, and resurrection; your way of life should at all times reflect the goodness of Christ." It continues, "Be active members of the Church, alive in Jesus Christ. . . . Give your lives completely in the service of all, as did Christ."[255]

Then, putting this exhortation into action, those to be confirmed renew their baptismal promises,[256] literally giving witness before the assembly. The first of the suggested general intercessions prays that the newly confirmed "give witness to Christ by lives built on faith and love."[257] The prayer over the people asks God, "keep the gifts of your Holy Spirit active in the hearts of your people. Make them ready to live his Gospel and eager to do his will. May they never be ashamed to proclaim to all the world Christ crucified living and reigning for ever and ever."[258]

An alternate opening prayer asks God, "send your Holy Spirit to make us witnesses before the world to the Good News proclaimed by Jesus Christ."[259] And a communion prayer asks that those anointed may "live in holiness and be your witnesses to the world."[260]

Thus, confirmation, a sacrament of initiation, strengthens one to become more like Christ and bear witness to the world.

The Holy Spirit

Confirmation is able to achieve this lofty goal because it is the sacrament whose primary purpose is to give the gift of the Holy Spirit. It celebrates the very presence and activity of God.

In confirmation, bishops hand on "the special gift of the Holy Spirit,"[261] as received by the apostles at Pentecost.

Although the comparison to Pentecost is frequently made, the liturgy admits that "in our day the coming of the Holy Spirit in confirmation is no longer marked by the gift of tongues, but we know his coming by faith." His presence is marked in other ways: "He fills our hearts with the love of God, brings us together in one faith but in different vocations, and works within us to make the Church one and holy."[262] The fruits of the Spirit are the unity of the church[263] and the holiness of its members.[264]

The ritual employs two important symbols of the Holy Spirit: the imposition of hands[265] and the anointing with chrism.[266] In the anointing with chrism Christians are "sealed with the gift of the Spirit."[267]

The liturgy highlights other parts of the Mass to underscore the theme of the Holy Spirit. When the candidates renew their baptismal promises, they find that the third one has been expanded: "Do you believe in the Holy Spirit, the Lord, the giver of life, who came upon the apostles at Pentecost and today is given to you sacramentally in confirmation?"[268] Emphasis is also given the liturgy of the Word since the Spirit flows from there, and reciting the Lord's Prayer, "because it is the Spirit who prays in us, and in the Spirit the Christian says '*Abba*, Father.' "[269]

The giving of the Spirit is the heart of the sacrament.

The Church

Another theme of the liturgy is the role of the church, the community. Confirmation sits in an ecclesial context, evidenced by its nature as initiation and the participation of the people.

As initiation, confirmation binds the candidate more closely to the church.[270] Preparation may imitate the catechumenate.[271] The ritual culminates in the symbols of community: the sign of peace and the eucharist.[272]

Members of the community play a role in the celebration. People and pastors alike help prepare the candidates.[273] Parents assist in the preparation of children.[274] Sponsors enjoy a range of responsibilities: they represent the community at large, they call the name of those to be confirmed, and they indicate their support by physically laying a hand on the candidate's shoulder.[275] They will continue a relationship after the celebration.[276] The bishop bonds the newly confirmed to the universal church.[277] And the whole assembly joins in the liturgy,[278] praying and singing.[279]

Adaptations are encouraged for the benefit of the assembly's role.[280]

The order raises pastoral concerns: that records be kept,[281] pastors remain informed,[282] and all preparations be made ready.[283]

Finally, the liturgy recalls the effect this sacrament has on the universal church: It will grow in unity,[284] strength,[285] and holiness.[286]

Origins

Finally, among the principal themes one finds in these texts arises an almost self-conscious concern to express the origins of confirmation.

The Apostolic Constitution eloquently sketches the background of confirmation in the life and mission of Jesus. The Spirit descended and remained with him, impelled him into public ministry, and assisted him throughout. The suggested homily for confirmation sounds the same theme. "At his baptism by John, Christ himself was anointed by the Spirit and sent out on his public ministry to set the world on fire."[287] The Constitution continues, "(Jesus) later promised his disciples that the Holy Spirit would help them also to bear fearless witness to their faith even before persecutors."

That promise became real on the day of Pentecost, an event all three documents recall.[288] The Acts of the Apostles records the deeds and preaching of the apostles as a result of this event. And, significantly, the Constitution tells how the apostles "imparted the gift of the Spirit to the newly baptized by the laying on of hands to complete the grace of baptism." The Constitution recalls that "the Letter to the Hebrews lists among the first elements of Christian instruction the teaching about baptism and the laying on of hands."[289]

This New Testament background sets the stage for interpreting the later practice of confirmation. The rite sees in the role of the bishop the continuation of the ministry of the apostles.[290] Priests who confirm in certain circumstances in the west do so by exception, or by participating in the work of the bishop.[291] Chrism used in the sacrament, no matter who the minister is in east or west, must be consecrated by a bishop.[292] And priests who assist the bishop in the rite receive the chrism directly from his hands.[293] If for some reason the bishop is not the principal celebrant of the liturgy, he should preside at the liturgy of the Word and give the final blessing.[294] All this intends to imitate the perception of New Testament times, that on Pentecost the apostles not only received the Spirit but also the power of giving the Spirit, that they did so by imposing hands on the baptized, and that bishops now succeed the apostles in this ministry. "Bishops are successors of the apostles and have this power of giving the Holy Spirit to the baptized, either personally or through the priests they appoint."[295]

Having established this scriptural context the Constitution sketches the history of confirmation in east and west. "These rites underwent many changes in the East and the West, while always keeping the significance of a conferring of the Holy Spirit." Examples include the variations in words and gestures. The Constitution concludes that today's ritual—anointing with chrism and speaking the words adapted from the Byzantine tradition—culminates the long tradition of conferring the Spirit originating in New Testament practice.

Concerns

The order of confirmation interprets the sacrament with remarkable internal cohesion. Concerns arise when comparing this rite to other models of confirmation, and with certain aspects of history.

Initiation

Although the documents highlight the importance of revising confirmation to make its place in initiation more evident, their consistency fails. The Decree which opens the documentation says that in confirmation, "the initiation in the Christian life is completed." The authors have in mind a sequence of initiation which places confirmation after eucharist. This is hard to justify with the Constitution which says confirmation's link with the sacraments of initiation should be shown by "closer association of these sacraments." The introduction to the order, in fact, implies that some may be confirmed before first eucharist.[296] The same passage points out the importance of receiving confirmation and eucharist together. And the Eastern Churches never separated chrismation from baptism.

This inconsistency in references to the sequence of the sacraments of initiation came about because the revised order of confirmation created a place for the confirmation of adolescents.[297] Annibale Bugnini says the age of confirmation became an important issue in the discussions preceding the revision.[298] Botte says Paul VI himself favored conferring the sacrament on adolescents.[299] The order now compromises by neither requiring one age nor forbidding a variation in the sequence of the sacraments.

Some dioceses have experimented in retaining the initiatory sequence for cases of deferred confirmation. For example, they might celebrate confirmation at first communion for children around the age of discretion.[300] Such a move restores the ancient sequence, but still raises the question about what confirmation means once it has been removed from the rites of baptismal initiation. If original sequence is so important, why defer confirmation at all? For that matter, why defer first communion? Many Eastern Rites have preserved the custom of giving communion to those baptized in infancy. Their practice questions why the western church "excommunicates" infants at the moment of baptism.

Celebrating confirmation before first communion gives children the same sequence of initiation sacraments that adults have when they join the church. However, sequence alone does not make confirmation initiation; its conjunction with baptism in the same ceremony drives the point home. Confirmation at age seven still recognizes some catechetical achievement—just as first eucharist at this age does. Hence, deferred confirmation—at any age and in any sequence—still feels more like a maturity rite than an initiation rite. Confirmation prior to first communion certainly helps to make the initiatory connection, but it imperfectly solves the problem of unifying the meaning of this sacrament.

The questions of sequence and age cast light on the meaning of initiation in the context of confirmation, as will be seen in the next chapter. Is initiation a beginning? Or a longer process of conversion? Another example of how this issue appears concerns the role of the sponsor for adult candidates for confirmation. According to Bugnini,[301] a discussion arose during the revisions whether or not adults needed a confirmation sponsor; one argument held that they could simply present themselves. Although the explicit permission is not given, the possibility remains when the introduction to the rite says, "Ordinarily there should be a sponsor," and "It is for the local Ordinary to determine diocesan practice in the light of local circumstances."[302] But without a sponsor, the community's role in initiation would be obscured. Further, this would nuance confirmation as a sacrament of personal achievement, a theme implicit in the deferment of confirmation, but not explicitly found elsewhere in the liturgy, even when it explains that one result of confirmation will be strengthening.

The various models for confirmation increasingly present a less unified interpretation of the sacrament. How ironic that the Constitution recalls that Vatican II "prescribed that the rites should be suitably revised in order to make them more suited to the understanding of the faithful." The National Catechetical Directory for Catholics of the United States laments how difficult it is to prepare for confirmation because "it is impossible to prescribe a single catechesis for this sacrament."[303]

Imposition of Hands

The Constitution boasts of the importance of the imposition of hands, but the symbol remains weak in the revised rite. Thankfully the Constitution avoids saying that chrism alone would suffice for confirmation. Still, the introduction to the rite regrettably admits that "the laying of hands . . . does not pertain to the valid giving of the sacrament." But for all the pains it takes to honor the tradition of imposing hands in history and even in apostolic practice, the gesture disappoints.

Traditionally two opportunities present themselves for the imposition of the hand: in accompanying the prayer or the anointing. The Constitution says the anointing is done "by the laying on of the hand." But the rite envisions the bishop will impose hands at the prayer by extending them over all the candidates at once,[304] and there is no mention of imposing a hand on the candidate's

head during the anointing. The Pontifical Commission for Interpreting the Decrees of Vatican II claimed that the anointing with
the thumb signified the imposition of hands![305]

The order strives hard to place confirmation against its scriptural background, but backs away from using the dominant
scriptural gesture for imparting the Holy Spirit: the imposition
of hands.

Minister

Increasingly, permissions are granted for priests to confirm.
Since Vatican II, a greater proportion of confirmations have been
performed by priests than at any other time in western history.
This development denotes a serious departure from the entire
tradition of this sacrament. From its beginnings as a separate ritual, confirmation belonged to the office of the bishop. The whole
point of delaying confirmation after baptism was to directly involve his ministry.

Today in the west, priests present at the confirmation of children may assist the bishop or even take his place. When they
baptize a child of catechetical age or adult, they confirm immediately. When they receive one's profession of faith they confirm
the new Catholic. The occasions for the bishop to confirm
have diminished, and many parishes may not see a bishop for
some years.

Formerly, when bishops felt overworked, they could petition
for the ordination of an auxiliary bishop simply to help the ministry of confirmation. This practice abused the office of bishop,
and realized once again Luther's complaint that confirmation's
purpose was simply to give bishops something to do.

Consequently, without the presence of the bishop, the symbol of his interest in initiation is reduced from his personal ministry to the parish jar of chrism. Since priests confirm on more
occasions, the independent rite of confirmation is now drifting
from its fifth century origins which connected children to the
diocesan church. This may not be bad, but it should be acknowledged, and evaluated. For the more priests are allowed to confirm,

the more the church will need a good explanation for not confirming infants at baptism.

Origins

In general, there are problems defining the origins of confirmation. In turning to the Scriptures, the Apostolic Constitution wisely offers Jesus as model of one filled with the Spirit who acts in the Spirit. But references to the imposition of hands in Acts of the Apostles wilt when invoked as the origins of confirmation. The intent of the apostles and the extent of the practice remains unknown. It is inappropriate to read all the modern themes of confirmation into this early record. The earliest Church Fathers who anointed the newly baptized never referred to these apostolic texts.[306] The Constitution claims, "This laying on of hands is rightly recognized by Catholic tradition as the beginning of the sacrament of confirmation, which in a certain way perpetuates the grace of Pentecost in the Church." It may rightly be "the beginning," but it's difficult to defend that it was "the sacrament" itself. The sacrament more clearly developed in later initiatory practice.

Practical Effects

Confirmation is expected or required for certain persons in the church. Candidates for marriage are expected to be confirmed.[307] Candidates for ordination[308] and for the novitiate[309] must be confirmed. Godparents for baptism[310] and sponsors for confirmation[311] must be confirmed; they should model Christian care.

However, one wonders what practical effect confirmation really has in these circumstances. Many sponsors are chosen because of relationship or influence. (This is more true of baptism than confirmation.) Since the marriage ministry of the church extends to the full range of members—from most active to least— some who apply for this sacrament won't know if they ever celebrated confirmation, nor how important canon law regards it for marriage, nor why. Many Christian role models who would perform admirably as confirmation sponsors may find themselves ineligible if they were never confirmed. Although the church expects its members to be confirmed, many members have not seen the value, and the pool of confirmed members remains much smaller than that of the baptized.

Does confirmation really matter to people? Theologically and canonically, yes it does. Practically, however, it often does not.

6

Adolescent Confirmation

Introduction

Confirming adolescents has become an increasingly common practice in the Catholic Church since the 1970's. Prior to this time children who were baptized in infancy generally were confirmed seven to twelve years later. Confirming thirteen to seventeen year olds has become widespread not just in the United States but in many countries throughout the world.

The confirmation of teens follows the same ritual text used for younger children. The ritual assumes that these children were baptized as infants when their confirmation was deferred. Although the church still regards confirmation as a "sacrament of initiation" in these circumstances,[312] it is displaced from the baptismal rites.

This chapter will explain why some people prefer the confirmation of adolescents, some of the arguments used to support their position, and some concerns.

Why Confirm Adolescents?

The Origins of Teenage Confirmation

The confirmation of adolescents has its origins in the experience of those charged with religious education and formation of teens. Parents and educators have long searched for a way to ensure religious formation. This search reveals a love for the church, a care for teens, and a fear that unassisted teens might

85

choose not to participate in the church's life. It is founded on the belief that sacraments should relate to the real experience of people.[313]

By the 1970's experiments in delaying confirmation to teen years were revealing positive results for this pastoral dilemma: Offering the sacrament as a goal created the opportunity for a formation program which supported a deeper involvement of teens in the church community. For those baptized as infants because of their parents' commitment to the church, confirmation ritualized their own commitment. Early results demonstrated to many catechists that confirmed teens persevered in their church membership.[314]

The origins of this framework for confirmation differ from the origins for other Catholic models. Confirmation for teens springs from a pastoral concern for those whose practice of the faith either has lessened or is imperiled. Confirmation of children began as a way of involving the bishop in the initiation rites. Confirmation of adults being baptized into the church and Eastern Rite chrismation came from a desire to highlight aspects of the meaning of baptism for those who are moving from one worldview into the Christian way of life.

Adolescent confirmation contrasts with the model of adult initiation: In the first case those to be confirmed have been Catholics for many years; in the other they are just joining the church. With adolescents, the community wishes to awaken a committed faith in the individual; with adults, the community wishes to celebrate the gift of the Holy Spirit in the newly initiated Christian, who already expressed his or her committed faith in baptism. Commitment, which is an important issue for the confirmation of adolescents, is not a consideration for the confirmation of adults joining the church; however, commitment is an extremely important issue for the *baptism* of adults joining the church.

The origins of adolescent confirmation, therefore, lie in the practical experience of catechists. However, there were other developments which fostered an environment in which this approach could flower. One goes back to the 1910 publication of *Quam singulari,* and others took place in the 1970's: the decision of the **United States bishops** regarding the age of confirmation, and the **evolution of catechetical theory.**

In 1910 the Sacred Congregation of Sacraments under Pope Pius X promulgated the decree *Quam singulari*,[315] which changed the age for the first reception of eucharist. At that time the customary age for first eucharist was teenage years. The Congregation moved the age down to seven. In doing so they corrected a situation which deprived children of communion, but they innocently created another problem: what to do with the age of confirmation. *Quam singulari* does not discuss confirmation, and by moving communion forward, it unwittingly displaced confirmation from its customary position. Suddenly the sequence of these two sacraments was reversed: confirmation followed eucharist, but no theological or pastoral reflection accompanied the practice. It took some decades for the impact to be realized, but eventually confirmation migrated out to the age left behind by first eucharist.[316]

The **American bishops** finally faced the question of age because the Catholic Church does not universally determine the age of confirmation for those who are baptized as infants. The *Rite of Confirmation* of 1971 states that

> the administration of confirmation is generally postponed until the seventh year. For pastoral reasons, however, especially to strengthen the faithful in complete obedience to Christ the Lord in loyal testimony to him, episcopal conferences may choose an age which seems more appropriate, so that the sacrament is given at a more mature age after appropriate formation.[317]

Thus, the decision regarding the age of confirmation falls to a conference of bishops. In the United States, all the bishops in the country form the conference, the National Conference of Catholic Bishops (NCCB).

The NCCB dealt with the question of a national age for confirmation on two occasions. The first was in 1972, in response to the publication of the new order of confirmation. The Committee on Pastoral Research and Practices discerned five possible ages for confirmation (prior to first eucharist, around sixth grade, adolescence, entrance to adulthood, and during adulthood), and observed that the pastoral climates in the United States were "varying." The Committee recommended that the NCCB not adopt an age different from the one stated in the *Rite of Confirmation* (seven), allowing any bishop "to set a later age as normative in his jurisdiction." The NCCB approved the proposal by a majority vote.[318]

In 1983 the revised code of canon law was published, reiterating the provision from the order of confirmation; namely, that confirmation is to be conferred

> at about the age of discretion unless the conference of bishops determines another age or there is danger of death or in the judgment of the minister a grave cause urges otherwise.[319]

In the 1917 code, "grave cause" always urged moving confirmation earlier, to assist in danger of death, for example.[320] The 1983 code remains ambiguous about which direction from seven "another age" might be.

The code also offered minimum requirements for confirmation:

> Outside the danger of death, to be licitly confirmed it is required, if the person has the use of reason, that one be suitably instructed, properly disposed and able to renew one's baptismal promises.[321]

The requirements were minimal, but they did not forbid choosing a later age.

The practice of confirming teens had gained widespread support in the United States by this time, but there was still no uniform practice: Individual dioceses celebrated confirmation for children from ages eight to seventeen. Because of the flexibility in canon law, the question about the proper age for confirmation appeared a second time for the NCCB's discussion in 1984.

Again, the bishops were unable to agree upon a national age for confirmation. This time the Pastoral Research and Practices Committee had specifically recommended grades 8–11 as the preferred age for administering the sacrament, freeing bishops to choose a different age for pastoral reasons. But after much discussion, the proposal did not pass. Instead, the bishops chose a solution which even the code of canon law technically did not fore-see:[322] They set no national age, and simply let each diocese choose its own.[323] Instead of determining another age as a confer-ence, as the code envisions, they decided to allow a wide range of ages to co-exist.[324] This is why Catholics of one diocese celebrate confirmation at one age, while neighbors in another diocese do so at a different age.

By allowing the co-existence of multiple confirmation ages the NCCB opened a window for the practice and theory of adoles-cent confirmation to develop. Although the conference did not determine a universal age for confirmation in the United States, they permitted the practice of adolescent confirmation.

Another factor that contributed to the growing practice of adolescent confirmation was the **evolution of catechetical theory**—or, the theory of how people best learn and grow in faith. The principal shift in theory has been from abstract learning to experiential learning, or from learning ideas in books to learn-ing ideas from one's experience.

An example of the former method is learning from a cate-chism. A common catechetical practice used to be memorizing answers to questions from a catechism. This learning of ideas gradually nurtured a growth in one's faith. But catechetical theory now maintains that people learn ideas better by reflecting on their personal experience of them. So religious growth begins with ask-ing how God has acted in one's own life, and then shapes one's reflection on that experience into concepts that form the back-bone of religious education. Both methods teach the faith and foster spiritual growth, but the method which acknowledges expe-rience helps the learner appropriate more directly and personally.[325]

This environment for religious formation—an environment which honors personal experience—provided fertile ground for adolescent confirmation. Teens who reflected on their life experi-ence deepened their personal involvement with faith. This they ritualized in a sacrament. Many theologians believed this put more teeth into the sacramental experience, removing its magical tendencies for those who celebrated sacraments without much interior renewal.[326] And educators reflecting on *their* experience with teens discerned that this was a new spirit-filled occasion in the church. They argued that even though the confirmation of teens never existed as a general practice in church history, their experience in the late twentieth century led them to believe that this should be the present and future direction of this sacrament.

What Adolescent Confirmation Is About

Put simply, the goal of adolescent confirmation is **commitment**. The means is **maturity**. The fruit is **witnessing** the faith.[327]

Commitment becomes the goal for adolescent confirmation because its candidates were baptized in infancy when their parents' commitment to the faith made them eligible for initiation. As the candidates grow older, they make many decisions about their lives, including decisions about how committed they are to their church community. They may approach church membership with more or less commitment than their parents possess.

Adolescent confirmation, then, works from the assumption that children reach a point where faith becomes their own, not another's, and they make a free choice to belong to the community that holds that same faith.[328]

This assumption also cautions lest children be forced into possessing faith or church membership. A free choice shows that they have appropriated faith for themselves.

This self-appropriation, then, is ritualized in a sacrament of the church. The desire for this ritualization arises both from the point of view of the teen and from that of the church. From the teen's point of view, self-appropriation marks a decisive point in his or her personal development. Such a point yearns for ritualization, to celebrate the achievement and to seal it. Graduation, awards banquets, and marriage proposals are examples of how society ritualizes a decisive point in an individual's development. Adolescent confirmation fulfills a similar need for the teen.

For the church, adolescent confirmation answers the church's desire to celebrate this sacrament with all the baptized. Sacraments make visible God's invisible presence in the life of the church. All the signs of the ritual express this presence, including the sign of the people celebrating the sacrament. In the case of confirmation, those to be confirmed are signs of the church in whom the Holy Spirit dwells. Their decisive commitment to their faith makes them more eloquent signs of God's presence.

The ritual itself echoes the rite of baptism. Since it marks a self-appropriation of baptismal faith, the ritual includes the renewal of baptismal promises, thus revivifying the mystery of baptism in the life of the believer.

The ritual is the same for the seven year old or the seventeen year old. The same texts are called upon to mean commitment or strengthening. By leaving the specific occasion for a child's confirmation undetermined, the church rendered the meaning of the ritual ambiguous.

The whole issue of commitment could stem from the reforms of the baptismal ritual. Vatican Council II created an order of baptism for children. Prior to the council, children were baptized in a ritual that shortened the form of adult baptism. It was never well adapted for infants: The presider asked the infants to state what they wanted from the church, to renounce Satan, and to profess their belief in the Trinity. The revised rite asks these questions of the parents and godparents. Baptizing infants demands the faith of a community who will receive them and nurture their spiritual growth. But it specifically requires a commitment to faith on the part of parents and godparents, and this commitment has been introduced into the rite of infant baptism.

It was absurd for the old rite to ask commitment from infants, but not asking for it left a vacuum. The church asks adult baptismal candidates for a commitment—when does the church hear commitment from children? If asking for baptism, renouncing Satan, and professing belief in the Trinity is part of a Christian's initiation, should these rituals find another place in the initiation process?

The practice of adolescent confirmation gained popularity as a way to fill this ritual vacuum. The renewal of baptismal promises in the context of confirmation accompanies a commitment from teens who now speak for themselves what their parents and godparents spoke for them when their faith was entrusted to the community.[329]

The baptism of infants in most Roman Catholic parishes today is an embarrassingly innocuous rite. Ordinarily baptisms take place after the assembly has been dismissed from the last Sunday Mass. A few family and friends gather around a small bowl in a corner of the church. The celebrant typically pours a trickle of water over the baby's head, dabs on a little chrism, and wipes both away with a cloth. The minimalization of baptismal symbols may foster a catechist's fear that infant baptism has little to do with membership.

Catechesis for confirmation grows in importance when it is interpreted as a rite of commitment. Clearly, if someone is preparing to commit to a cause, he or she should understand the cause. "Catechesis" implies not just knowledge, but moral formation. The task of catechesis for adolescent confirmation, then, is to ensure the moral and intellectual formation of those seeking to speak their own faith commitment.

Maturity is the means by which the goal of commitment is achieved. Christian maturity implies accomplishing a certain level of catechesis which enables one to commit to the church.[330]

This demand for maturity takes on significant proportions when one considers that the church requires baptism, confirmation, and eucharist for full initiation. The maturity required of a seven year old for confirmation is considerably less than that required of a seventeen year old. In fact, the maturity required for first communion is considerably less than for adolescent confirmation. What adolescent confirmation introduces in history is the demand that to be fully initiated all Christians must attain a more adult level of maturity and commitment. One could argue that for nearly two thousand years of church history, an infant born of a Christian household and baptized into the church was never asked to profess an adult level of faith—until the last few decades.[331] Adolescent confirmation makes a higher level of maturity a prerequisite for full initiation into the church.

This maturity bears fruit in a stronger **witness** to the faith. This may be the only uniform element implied in all models of confirmation. Those who celebrate the gift of the Holy Spirit carry that gift with them in living and professing the Christian life.[332]

Thomas Aquinas defined the character of confirmation in these terms. He argues that baptism provides "the power to do those things which pertain to one's own salvation," but confirmation provides "the power to do those things which pertain to the spiritual fight against the enemies of the faith."[333] Thus the specific sacramental character of confirmation confers a power to confess the faith publicly. Sacraments which cannot be repeated are said to impart a "character," or a permanent mark or brand on the Christian. This is related to the concept of the "seal" in the theology of chrismation. According to Aquinas, it is the very irrepeatable nature of confirmation which empowers one to bear witness for the church.

It's interesting to compare the importance of maturity and witness in Catholic adolescent confirmation to the theology of confirmation in Protestant churches. The Reform professed the doctrine of "justification by faith alone"; that is, that salvation is God's gift for those who have faith; one's good works cannot of themselves gain salvation. In these churches, confirmation recognizes a level of catechesis. For the Catholic Church, adolescent confirmation generally requires "good works" (or "service projects") for the demonstration of faith and for full initiation into the church. Surprisingly, similar requirements appear in the pastoral practice of Protestant churches, even though their theological emphasis rests on faith. Thus, Catholics and Protestants both celebrate a delayed confirmation, and preparation for the celebration emphasizes service and faith for both.

Confirmation as Initiation

Since confirmation is one of the sacraments of initiation into the Catholic Church, its celebration so many years after baptism calls for clarifications of its role in initiation and its relationship to eucharist.

The principal difference in adolescent confirmation is that it completes the process of initiation, a process which is completed by eucharist in the models of adult initiation and the Eastern Rites.

In adult initiation, the process may be summarized in stages: 1) evangelization and conversion, 2) catechesis, 3) baptism, confirmation, and first eucharist.

However, in adolescent confirmation, the process may be described as follows: 1) infant baptism, 2) evangelization and catechesis, 3) first eucharist, 4) conversion, 5) confirmation.[334]

Here the initiation rites have become a long process, marked by different stages, culminating in one's commitment, or conversion of heart, ritualized in confirmation. This approach to initiation requires a faith commitment as the end of the process for those baptized in infancy.[335] It states that initiation is incomplete without it.[336] Further, it states that that commitment culminates the process of initiation, making one a full member of the body of Christ. Initiation is thus not simply the beginning of one's relationship with the church—it includes a long-sought-for intentional relationship with the church, resulting from the self-appropriation of one's faith.

Eucharist plays a different role in the initiation process when this is the case. Eucharist nurtures adolescents all their lives and accompanies them on their journey to confirmation. One could argue that fully initiated members celebrate eucharist in a richer sacramental experience after confirmation, but eucharist is not the climax of initiation as it is for adult initiation. That falls to confirmation.[337]

Possible Futures

Adolescent confirmation has developed so recently that its evolution may not be complete. Because its theology is based on experience with young people, its meaning and celebration may change as freely as experiences do.

The literature is diverse. Since human experience varies from one situation to another, one author's point of view may differ substantially from others. For as brief a time as the custom has been in practice, theological reflection on adolescent confirmation is surprisingly active. Still, the literature remains in a state of flux, and its future is undetermined. Will it emphasize service? The Holy Spirit? Church membership? It's just too early to tell.

A significant issue has arisen in considering the future. Some theologians advocate that confirmation be made a repeatable celebration.[338] This acknowledges that the experience of commitment happens over and over in life, and that life's stages are sanctified when they can be ritualized.

One also faces the problem of those who were baptized as children of catechetical age. They are confirmed at baptism, often long before their adolescent years. If adolescence is the age of commitment, then some ritual would still be needed for those who have already been confirmed. Theoretically, the same would apply to members of Eastern Rites: Chrismated as infants, they have no teen rite of commitment. Another possible future for confirmation, then, is to provide some ritual experience for adolescents who were already confirmed as children.

Further Arguments

Although the rationale for adolescent confirmation began largely with the experience of youth ministers, further arguments have come forth. These include the testimony of history and the Scriptures; passages in the order of Christian initiation of adults, the order of baptism for children, and the order of confirmation; and the experience and reflection of diverse cultures and theologians.

History

Some aspects of the history of confirmation support its celebration as a ritual distinct from baptism. This can be seen from the developments of the fifth century.

As explained earlier, the term "confirmation" is used for the first time in history in fifth century Gaul to describe the role of the bishop in his ceremony with children who were baptized by presbyters.[339]

One could argue that the origins of adolescent confirmation lie here in fifth century Gaul, not in early initiation rituals. Before this time, the imposition of hands and anointing with oil usually accompanied baptism. But the ceremony was not called "confirmation" in these early integral baptismal liturgies prior to the fifth century. Only when confirmation got its own occasion (the arrival of the bishop on a day other than Easter to areas he may visit only once in several years) did it develop its own rite and title. Since adolescent confirmation is so separate from infant baptism its origins stem more from this fifth century separate rite than from the second and third century integral initiation rites.

Already in the fifth century there were four different models of confirmation: confirmation as part of adult initiation (which was on the wane in the west), confirmation/chrismation of all ages in the baptismal rituals of the east, the anointing which accompanied the reconciliation of heretics, and now the bishop's confirmation of children who had been baptized by presbyters. This latest development, the bishop's confirmation of children, was so radically different, that the independent "confirmation" of today simply did not exist prior to this time.[340]

Through many centuries, confirmation resembled a many-headed creature. Although its dominant form in the west celebrated the gift of the Holy Spirit for young children, it shared kinship with chrismation in the east and adult initiation rites in the west. This multiplicity of meanings and occasions provided an environment in which one or more new interpretations of the sacrament might find tolerant company.

The restoration of the catechumenate in Vatican II also restored confirmation to its pre-fifth century situation, integral with the rites of baptism. But by the late twentieth century, the tradition for separating confirmation from baptism enjoyed a long history. Neither of these time-honored traditions could displace the other. The ritual books of Vatican II honored this twofold approach.

The co-existence of two occasions for the same ritual might have proved an embarrassment for the church, but it serves to acknowledge that the initiation of adults differs from that of children. The school of adolescent confirmation believes that the difference concerns commitment to the faith, a pastoral notion that the liturgical books treat in the baptismal vows ("Do you renounce . . . ? Do you believe . . . ?"). If confirmation was to fill the vacuum of faith commitment, it seemed more appropriate to delay its celebration further to an age and occasion when real commitment was possible.

Although the notion of confirming teens is new in history, it follows from the evolution of confirmation, a process that began in the fifth century when it first separated from baptism. Fittingly, since confirmation is the sacrament of the Holy Spirit *par excellence*, some argue that that Spirit is only now leading the church to a new form of the sacrament.

Do sacraments change dramatically in history? Some do and some don't. The rites of marriage and reconciliation have endured substantial changes throughout history.[341] Baptism and eucharist,

on the other hand, have seen little theological change and accepted minor ritual adjustments over the centuries. So, could confirmation be continuing a natural historical evolution? Proponents of the school of adolescent confirmation believe the answer
is clear. Yes it could be. Yes it is.[342]

Scripture

Once confirmation separated from baptism, theologians un-
derstandably turned to the Scriptures to look for verification.
Theologians since the fifth century have studied the Acts of the
Apostles to support the practice of confirming children some
years after they were baptized.[343]

Predictably, now that confirmation is undergoing further historical development, theologians turn to the Scriptures for support. Once again, Acts of the Apostles proves popular.

Two famous scenes in Acts show an imposition of hands
upon new Christians on an occasion distinct from baptism. Acts 8,
14–17, tells that Samaritans have been baptized, but Peter and
John arrive to lay hands on them and then they receive the Holy
Spirit. Acts 19, 1–7 relates that Ephesians have been baptized, but
Paul arrives to lay hands on them and then they receive the Holy
Spirit. These two classic texts have fueled the confirmation debate
for centuries. They were heavily interpreted and reinterpreted in
the controversies after the sixteenth century Reformation.[344]

These two rituals, baptism and the imposition of hands, have
supported the practice of initiating in two steps—the one baptismal, the other pertaining to the gift of the Holy Spirit.[345]

In canvassing the New Testament for additional support, one
must consider St. Paul. Of all the authors, Paul wrote most exten-
sively on baptism and the Holy Spirit, but remains surprisingly
silent about any imposition of hands following baptism. Paul's
silence is just that: silence. Perhaps he had no knowledge of imposing hands on the baptized as part of initiation. Perhaps he
simply abbreviates his references to this complex rite: Rather than
mentioning all the component parts of initiation, Paul speaks of
them under the single unitive title of baptism.[346] Perhaps Paul
ignores the imposition of hands because his interest is theological,
not liturgical; thus, he does not offer all the information later
liturgists want to know.[347]

What Scripture does say is that those who wished to join the Christian community did so in rites of initiation, that baptism was the primary initiation rite, that the gift of the Holy Spirit became manifest in Christians, and that the imposition of hands imparted that gift on two occasions.[348]

The Order of Christian Initiation of Adults

Proponents of adolescent confirmation find additional support in contemporary liturgical books. The first of these is the order of Christian initiation of adults. It may surprise that this book could support the practice of adolescent confirmation. After all, adult initiation celebrates confirmation with baptism in every instance, and the adolescent model separates it by several years. But the two models may converge on some underlying principles of initiation.[349]

These principles are outlined when the order of Christian initiation of adults speaks about the period of the catechumenate —the time after one has expressed the desire for church membership, but prior to baptism.[350] First, there should be a catechesis to acquaint catechumens with the teachings of the church and the mystery of salvation. Second, it should introduce the Christian way of life. Third, liturgical rites should celebrate one's progress. And fourth, catechumens should begin spreading the Gospel by their words and actions.

Although these four principles are outlined for those who have not yet been baptized, they provide guidance for catechizing those already in the Christian way of life. Once baptized, Christians are not finished. They constantly need catechesis, moral formation, liturgical support, and the challenge to evangelize.

The model of confirmation for adolescents adopts these principles but changes their goal. Catechetical formation preparing adolescents to commit their lives to the church in confirmation is similar to catechetical formation preparing adults to commit their lives to the church in baptism, but the goal for adolescents is to persevere in Christian life. For adults, the goal is to begin the Christian life.

What underlies the application of these four principles is that catechesis takes a lifetime. More than learning about religion, more than preparing for a sacrament, catechesis nourishes a healthy Christian life, as exercise and a proper diet nourish a healthy human life. Adolescents preparing for the responsibilities of adulthood especially need the attentive sustenance of good catechesis. Confirmation of teens ritualizes both the catechesis and the maturity which accompany their journey into Christian adulthood.

Other Documentation

Other documentation can be found in the order of confirmation, the order of baptism for children, the code of canon law, and Vatican II's Constitution on the Sacred Liturgy.

In the *Rite of Confirmation* several passages apply. Frequently, the ritual uses language of a comparative degree. This has been noted above in adult initiation. For example, the bishop asks the assembly to pray that God will anoint the candidates to make them "more like Christ."[351] The introduction to the rite describes the anointing in a similar way.[352] It's tempting to assume that such comparative terms imply a maturity gained in time.[353]

Later the introduction speaks about the difference in preparing children and adults for confirmation.[354] Those with the use of reason must "be in a state of grace, properly instructed, and able to renew (their) baptismal promises." However,

> with regard to adults, the same principles should be followed, with suitable adaptations, which are in effect in individual dioceses for the admission of catechumens to baptism and the eucharist. In particular, suitable catechesis should precede confirmation, and there should be sufficient effective relationship of the candidates with the Christian community and with individual members of the faithful to assist in their formation. This formation should be directed toward their giving the witness of a Christian life and exercising the Christian apostolate, while developing a genuine desire to participate in the eucharist (cf. *RCIA* 75).[355]

Thus, adult preparation for confirmation should resemble the preparation of a catechumen for baptism, with suitable adaptations. Adults should relate as members of the Christian community, engage in catechesis, and be able to give witness to the Christian life while expressing a desire for eucharist.[356] These principles seem directed toward baptized but uncatechized adults preparing for both confirmation and eucharist,[357] but advocates of adolescent confirmation have interpreted them to apply to the formation of teens baptized in infancy.[358]

The Decree announcing the publication of the new rite and its replacement of the old states that in the sacrament of confirmation, "the initiation in the Christian life is completed." Since confirmation is one of the three sacraments of initiation, the Decree seems to assume that it will follow the celebration of first eucharist.

A similar assumption can be detected in the code of canon law when it considers catechesis in the church's ministry. It says that pastors should make provision "that children are properly prepared for the first reception of the sacraments of penance and Most Holy Eucharist and the sacrament of confirmation by means of a catechetical formation given over an appropriate period of time."[359]

Although the code generally refers to the sacraments of initiation in the order of their celebration for adults (baptism, confirmation, eucharist),[360] here when addressing the needs of children, the canon assumes that the order will be baptism, eucharist, and then confirmation.[361]

The order of baptism for children introduces its topic by stressing the importance of baptizing children, since it has long been the practice of the church, and since children should not be deprived of baptism. Then it urges that children must grow in the faith in which they are baptized:

> To fulfill the true meaning of the sacrament, children must later be formed in the faith in which they have been baptized. The foundation of this formation will be the sacrament itself, which they have already received. Christian formation, which is their due, seeks to lead them gradually to learn God's plan in Christ, so that they may ultimately accept for themselves the faith in which they have been baptized.[362]

Thus the *Rite of Baptism for Children* envisions that formation will follow baptism, and it will lead to acceptance of the faith. Many urge that that acceptance of faith be accompanied with a ritual celebration—namely, confirmation.[363]

Vatican II's Constitution on the Sacred Liturgy expressed the church's desire that the faithful come to a "full, conscious, and active participation" in the liturgy, to which they have a right and obligation by reason of their baptism.[364] One could argue that in order to fully participate at the eucharist, the baptized need to approach it with catechetical formation and commitment.[365] If true, celebrating the liturgy would assume the formation and commitment that adolescent confirmation seeks to make firm.[366]

In general, the liturgy of confirmation celebrates the participation of those to be confirmed in the broader life of the church. It stresses the role of Christian witness, and assures the presence of the Holy Spirit. These themes fit the situation of teens coming to maturity about the commitments in their lives.

Cross-Cultural Verification

Confirming adolescents establishes a goal which many educators believe is verifiable: committed Catholics. The goal is more easily verifiable when the candidates are beyond the traditional ages of seven to twelve years.

Adolescent confirmation has attained a cross-cultural appeal. In the United States, many anglo-saxons, blacks, hispanics, and native Americans find this model fits their experience.

Teen confirmation programs offer hispanics a useful organization for youth ministry. The quest for commitment is less an issue in this culture, arguably one of the most "committed" of Catholic cultures in its almost universal popular religiosity.

The goal for confirmation among hispanics is the goal for youth ministry in general: to provide catechetical formation. However, problems arise from the scarcity of confirmation materials in Spanish. Many hispanic communities adapt the English materials, which might help or hurt. It may hurt if it leads to inadequate catechesis in the hands of the unskilled translator. But it may help develop a process personalized to the local community, permitting it to prepare young people its own way. Developing pride in hispanic identity, the preferential option for the poor, and the promise of liberation theology can all be starting points for catechesis toward Christian maturity.[367]

Hispanics in the United States are themselves a multicultural group. Some have lived on the same land for centuries; others are recent immigrants. Some speak English; some do not. They represent diverse latin cultures. Mixing English-speaking hispanics with an anglo group or combining all Spanish speakers together does not respect the variety of cultures. Catechetical materials have not yet diversified to proper cultural adaptation.

The hispanic experience in the U.S. should not be confused with the confirmation customs of Mexico. Some places in Mexico retain the custom of confirming infants shortly after their baptism. This custom began centuries ago when the first missionaries to Mexico obtained permission to confirm infants in a country where bishops were scarce and baptisms numerous. Many of today's parents believe in the spiritual power of baptism and confirmation and do not want their children deprived of either. A bishop today may confirm infants of families in the city at his cathedral, or he may travel to rural areas and confirm two and three year olds. Some bishops allow priests to confirm infants, but the people prefer a bishop.

Occasionally, hispanic parents from the United States may travel to Mexico for the baptism and confirmation of their children. This allows families in separate countries to be together for the celebration, and assures the spiritual celebrations that popular piety holds so dear. A culture with a history of high infant mortality generates families who fear their children could die without all their sacraments. Sacraments assure them of God's grace and protection. And the godparents of the children will provide security in case the parents cannot.

However, in spite of this cultural tradition in Mexico, confirming teens seems to appeal to hispanics in the United States for the benefits of personal commitment and of participating in the local customs of this country.

A similar experience can be observed with native Americans. Many of them share a history of infant confirmation for the same reason as hispanics: Missionaries received permission from the

Vatican to confirm infants in regions where bishops were scarce. But the practice grew into a custom that many preferred to keep, notably among the Pueblos.

Today, however, the trend for native Americans is to follow the practice of the diocese in which they reside. So if confirming teens is local custom, it becomes native American custom as well. Since the original condition for infant confirmation has changed (the non-availability of bishops), adolescent confirmation becomes a way in which native Americans can take part more fully in the local life of the church.

The practice of infant confirmation among mission countries in the west calls to mind the practice in the east. The reason priests chrismated infants in the fifth century east is virtually the same reason the practice developed for hispanics and native Americans over a thousand years later: a shortage of bishops in a growing and diversifying church. The difference is that the Eastern Rites maintained the custom of having the priest who baptizes chrismate the infants.

The Eastern Rites have no adolescent rite of commitment which exactly parallels the growing phenomenon in the west.[368] Petras admits "a genuine ratification of the decision made for us at Baptism" would benefit adolescents of Eastern Rites. "That young people are capable and willing to make this recommitment is obvious," he continues, "for without them the Church would not survive."[369] Infant confirmation is no guarantee of later commitment.

Thus, teenage confirmation appeals to many cultures in the United States as either a verifiable ritual of the self-appropriation of the faith, or a useful youth ministry program.

Other Theologians

Tracing the writings on confirmation over the last half of the twentieth century, one sees many theologians who laid groundwork for delaying this sacrament toward teenage years.[370]

Writing in the 1960's, before the practice of adolescent confirmation became popular, Karl Rahner and Edward Schillebeeckx explained confirmation not as part of a single initiation rite, but as a separate celebration. The liturgical renewal was just beginning at this time and the order of Christian initiation of adults had not yet been published. Schillebeeckx saw baptism and confirmation representing the mysteries of Easter and Pentecost in the life of the Christian. "Both sacraments form an organic and living whole: one rite of initiation made up of two essential sacramental elements (which may therefore be separated in time)."[371] Rahner said "the beginning of adolescence is to be considered a suitable age for confirmation."[372] This simply acknowledged the practice of the time, confirming children as a kind of puberty rite at the beginning of adolescence, rather than when adolescence and teen years were in full flower.

In 1975 Piet Fransen argued that "there are grave pastoral reasons in some countries for confirming children only when they are about to become adults."[373] Francois-Xavier Durrwell wrote, "If baptism is given in early infancy, there would seem to be a place for deferring confirmation until an age when personal potential for virtue is developed."[374] And Juan Segundo worries about a semi-magical conception of the sacraments prevalent in cultures which offer too many sacraments too quickly for children too young: "Baptism, confirmation, and Holy Eucharist should mark stages of increasing participation, and respect the gradual rhythm of human life."[375]

Given this background, it is not surprising that in the 1980's several writers stated far more boldly the case for adolescent confirmation. Yves Congar acknowledges that confirmation

> emerges clearly as a personal ratification of the baptismal commitment. . . . If the logic of this option is to be fully respected, I would say confirmation should undoubtedly take place after puberty, when the young person's ways of feeling and perceiving reality are so fundamentally changed and the way is opened to an autonomous understanding of himself, and he is on the inevitable threshold of adult life.[376]

Congar believes a sacramental seal should be celebrated at baptism, but a later ritual of confirmation may accompany a more adult consciousness.

Bernard Cooke writes,

there is a deeper sharing of the Spirit only if there is truly an increased sharing of Christian faith and life by the community that celebrates confirmational liturgy, and if the candidates for confirmation are truly open to living according to the Spirit and to fulfilling the responsibilities of Christian adulthood.[377]

He further argues that more than one liturgy could be celebrated "as confirmation of the baptismal choice."[378]
Rembert Weakland argues that confirmation

permits the recipients to place themselves consciously in God's loving care as they utter, to the best of their ability and with all the insecurity that characterizes the human condition, their yes to him. It also permits them . . . to express their "belongingness" to a larger body, the church—and it permits the community to express its encouragement to them in its own act of faith.[379]

Finally, Kieran Sawyer strongly contrasts baptism and confirmation:

Baptism is seen as a beginning, as a first step in the initiation process; while confirmation is seen as the completion or fruition of that same baptismal commitment. Baptism, especially of infants, focuses on the faith of the church; confirmation focuses on the faith of the individual and on the role that the newly confirmed will assume in the ecclesial community. Baptism focuses on the gift dimension of the grace reality, on the unmerited bestowal of God's love on the baptized; confirmation focuses on the human response to grace—acceptance, gratitude, and commitment. Baptism is a celebration of the Easter mystery—the foundation of the church, the seed time, the first fruits; confirmation is a celebration of Pentecost—the continuation and growth of the church, the fullness of the harvest. Baptism focuses on Christ; confirmation focuses on the Spirit.[380]

This survey only begins to show the depth of reflection on this topic. The pattern emerging recalls what happened in the fifth century: After a new practice of confirmation was established, a theology developed to support it. The literature continues to multiply.

Concerns

As a newcomer in a two thousand year old church, adolescent confirmation could expect to meet skepticism. Yet every opposing argument has spawned more in favor. But the concerns are real.

Pastoral Theology

The adolescent confirmation school styles itself a pastoral approach to a theological problem. It interprets confirmation from practical contemporary experience, not from the niceties of historical consistency. By claiming that confirmation concerns commitment, this school contrasts the meaning of confirmation with the meaning preferred by what it calls the "historical" or "liturgical" school, who argue that confirmation in itself has nothing to do with commitment, but rather serves to highlight baptismal initiation.[381]

However, good sacramental theology requires knowledge of history and of current pastoral situations. Dividing into schools oversimplifies the complications of the meaning of confirmation. To imply that historical theology is not pastoral is to misunderstand historical theology. It, too, grew from pastoral considerations. To say one is "for pastoral theology" is a little like saying one is "pro-choice" or "pro-life": It's a pleasing way to package one's position. Everyone is "for pastoral theology," but pastoral theology encompasses much more than attention to the hapless predicaments of adolescents. It also commands responsible governance of symbols.

Confirming adolescents may also be criticized for stretching confirmation's practice too thin. It already fulfills several needs in the church: adult initiation, Eastern Rite chrismation, and symbol of unity under the diocesan bishop. Is it wise for this same ritual to now cover the commitment of teens? Besides, the non-commitment of teens can be documented in any age of history. It is not clear why twentieth century teens need a commitment ritual more than fifth century teens did. And if teens need a ritual to accompany a renewed commitment, is confirmation the best one for it?

Opportunities for ritual commitment already abound: the renewal of baptismal promises at Easter, liturgies of the Word, celebrations of penance in its many forms, blessings, and popular devotions. But those who minister to teens seem fearful that if a non-sacramental ritual of recommitment were offered to teens, they would not bother with it. Still, commitment which depends on a sizable reward may be commitment to a sacrament but not necessarily to personal faith.

Further, the desire for commitment originates not from teens but from committed parents and leaders. The goal of self-appropriating faith is hindered by the very process that seeks it: The parents, godparents, and church leaders who made the commitment at the time of infant baptism are the same ones orchestrating the commitment years later. Self-appropriation is difficult to measure.[382]

The desire for commitment comes at different points in life. Not all will sense the desire as teens. Some will do so earlier, some much later. Adolescent confirmation assumes that teens universally require a commitment ritual; that may not be true.

Finally, if experience is a starting point, one also needs to attend to the experience of the Eastern Rites. For two thousand years they have celebrated chrismation with baptism, and suffered no greater loss of commitment than western churches. Further, their baptismal rites have been enriched with the initiatory chrismation that has been impoverished in the west. To wrest chrismation away from baptism would violate two thousand years of experience and an honored sacramental tradition. To offer a second kind of confirmation would weaken the purpose of chrismation.

Terminology

Perhaps the greatest roadblock to resolving the dilemma of confirmation in the Catholic Church is that theologians do not use terms consistently. "Initiation," "catechumenate," "evangelization," "conversion," and "confirmation" itself are words that carry quite different meanings depending on who's arguing what point.

Most everyone agrees that confirmation is a sacrament of "initiation." But just what is initiation? An event? A process? A lifetime? Is it joining the church at the Easter Vigil? Or does it include the whole catechumenate? And for those baptized as infants, does it include delayed confirmation? Deathbed confirmation?

The problem with the term "initiation" is that two different models of initiation are at work in the debate over the age and occasion of confirmation. The adult model of initiation describes movement from non-membership to membership. The adolescent model of confirmation describes movement from partial to full membership. Adult baptism grafts new members onto the church; infant baptism generates new members within the church.[383]

Those who define confirmation according to the adult model find it difficult to see how adolescent confirmation can still be called initiation when candidates have experienced up to seventeen years of church membership since baptism, including the privilege of receiving communion, the church's most treasured symbol of membership. The inability to speak about "initiation" in universally acceptable terms can make it sound like those proposing adolescent confirmation as a rite of "initiation" claim that infant baptism is at least incomplete and at worst simply doesn't count.

To say that initiation is a lifelong process dilutes the meaning of baptismal initiation, which already celebrates membership in the body of Christ. Baptism makes a decisive difference in one's life. Once celebrated, there's no turning back, whether or not confirmation follows.

Similarly, the term "catechumenate" is used in unclear comparisons, as by those who attempt to model confirmation programs on the catechumenate. Precisely, in the order of Christian initiation of adults, catechumens are those in formation for baptism. Any time one hears of a process "modeled on the catechumenate," it's important to know in what sense. If that means that catechesis and prayer form part of the process, fine. But the catechumenate also means introducing someone to Christian community, renouncing a way of life known as non-Christian, and preparing for baptism. No process should bear that burden except the catechumenate itself. If the church models its catechesis for Christians on structures which assume they are not Christian, it has chosen the wrong process.[384]

Even more troublesome is "evangelization." In the order of Christian initiation of adults, "evangelization" refers to the period prior to the catechumenate, prior to the time people have decided whether or not the Catholic Church interests them. In the catechumenate, evangelization implies that people know so little about the Gospel they don't know what they want.

It's a term, however, used in Christianized settings. Pope Paul VI's encyclical, *Evangelization in the Modern World*, expands the notion of the term.[385] For Paul, evangelization is proclaiming the core of the Gospel message to Christians and non-Christians alike. That message is this:

> In Jesus Christ who became human, died, and rose again from the dead, salvation is offered to everyone as the gift of the grace and mercy of God.[386]

The goal is a universal proclamation of the Gospel:

> Evangelization means the carrying forth of the good news to every sector of the human race so that by its strength it may enter into the hearts of all people and renew the human race.[387]

Since for Paul evangelization refers to the action of proclaiming the Gospel and the subject matter it entails, the recipients of evangelization include even the church itself:

> If the church is to preserve the freshness, the ardor and the strength of its own work of preaching the Gospel it must itself be continuously evangelized.[388]

To say that "evangelization" is part of ministry to teens is no problem if one takes Paul VI's interpretation. But if speaking of "initiating teens," the term borrows the narrower definition of adult initiation, where "evangelization" assumes that candidates have no Christian background whatsoever. If a teen candidate for confirmation truly has little or no formation in the Gospel, the problem originated with the improper decision to baptize the infant into a nuclear Christian family which treated its obligations so lightly. But if teens do have some introduction to Christianity —indeed, if they are *receiving communion* in the church—"evangelization" as understood in the context of initiation is not the correct term. "Catechesis" may be better.

"Conversion" follows a similar pattern. The NCCB's National Statutes for the Catechumenate say "the term 'convert' should be reserved strictly for those converted from unbelief to Christian belief and never used of those baptized Christians who are received into the full communion of the Catholic Church."[389] By strictest definition, "conversion" is the interior process which accompanies baptism, not reception into full communion (for a Lutheran or Methodist, for example), and not confirmation. To call confirmation a conversion experience is to use the term analogously.

Outside the initiatory context, "conversion" may apply by analogy to the regenerated spiritual life of every Christian, the continuous process of inner renewal. In this sense, conversion happens every day and all life long, just like evangelization.

It's no surprise, then, that the word "confirmation" creates a problem in terminology. Is it a sacrament of adult initiation? Or is it a sacrament of a child's initiation into the broader Christian community represented by the bishop? Or is it a sacrament of a teen's commitment? These circumstances are all quite different. Expecting one term to cover all these instances invites havoc, misunderstanding, anger, and division.

All those involved in sacramental catechesis laudably strive for a common language. But when the terms are used imprecisely, or defined differently, they divide more than they unite.

Theology of Baptism

As indicated above, a theology of adolescent confirmation that stresses it completes infant baptism runs perilously close to saying that those baptized as infants are not initiated at all unless they are also confirmed. This would gravely misinterpret the effects of baptism as recognized by most major Christian churches in the world.[390] Further, to imply that the baptized are not initiated raises serious questions about the church's fidelity to the teachings of St. Paul himself. This is no small matter.

One argument cited above for the confirmation of teens points to the passage in the order of baptism for children which states that children should "ultimately accept for themselves the faith in which they have been baptized."[391] Although this acceptance remains a goal of catechesis, the order nowhere suggests that acceptance is a particular moment in the life of the child, nor that that moment should be ritualized, nor that the ritual should be confirmation. Acceptance of the faith is simply a goal of catechesis.

Membership Requiring Commitment

A sticky problem arises when the school of adolescent confirmation insists that church membership requires commitment. The ideal of a committed membership stems from the goals of the catechumenate. But transferring the desire for commitment to those already baptized raises several concerns. This section will explore four points: the occasions when commitment is waived, the danger of elitism, the problems of catechesis, and the implications of infant baptism for membership.

1) There are instances when the church in a sense waives the requirement of commitment for membership. The most obvious is infant baptism, since commitment has already been demonstrated in the faith of the family and the community that the baby is joining. The baby is being born into a Christian environment. That's different from a catechumen coming from a non-Christian, uncatechized background. Some infants will grow up to be fully committed members; others will not. But socially, canonically, and sacramentally they will be treated as baptized Christians forever: Their family and friends will regard them as Christian and share faith with them. The canon laws governing marriage, for example, extend certain obligations to baptized Catholics regarding the form of the marriage ceremony and the expectation of training children in the faith. Sacramentally, once a person is bap-

tized, he or she may never be baptized again. Baptism also opens the door to receiving the other sacraments. The commitment of the candidates for infant baptism is simply not required for their membership in the church.

Even the requirements for the parents' commitment are minimal. The Sacred Congregation for the Doctrine of the Faith wrote in its "Instruction on Infant Baptism" that parents who have little faith or practice their religion only occasionally, and seek baptism for an infant, need to give assurance that the child will receive the benefit of a Christian upbringing. The instruction says that "any pledge giving a well-founded hope for the Christian upbringing of the children deserves to be considered as sufficient."[392]

The code of canon law imitates this language when it allows infant baptism if there is a "founded hope that the infant will be brought up in the Catholic religion."[393] The code's requirement for participating in confirmation is that "the person has the use of reason, that one be suitably instructed, properly disposed and able to renew one's baptismal promises."[394] The requirements for confirmation retain the minimal spirit as those for baptism. The code suggests that confirmation be at the "age of discretion." That's a limited degree of maturity. The impulse of the code is to share the sacrament, to see that the faithful are not deprived of it.

Besides infant baptism, there are other cases where commitment is waived: The developmentally disabled are incapable of the kind of commitment described for adolescent confirmation, yet they may celebrate baptism, confirmation, eucharist, reconciliation, and anointing of the sick.[395] In fact, canon law gives them the same eligibility for baptism that infants enjoy,[396] and excuses them from the preparations required for confirmation.[397] Children in danger of death before adolescence do not have the opportunity or the inner maturity for that commitment either. The point here is that the church does not absolutely require maturity and commitment for sacraments of initiation in the same way it does for marriage or orders. Although many are mentally incapable of sacramental marriage or orders, baptism, confirmation, and eucharist are offered to those with less mental capacity. The pastoral tradition of the church has not been so strict to deny membership through the sacraments of initiation to those incapable of a strong commitment.

2) Claiming that commitment is required for confirmation threatens to limit church membership to a certain elite. Throughout history the church has lamented that many members do not live out their commitment, but it never organized a wholesale change in eligibility based on commitment. The fact is that there are many degrees of commitment represented in the church. Every parish roster lists the names of people whose participation in parish life ranges from daily to never. Humans fail in their ability to commit. A church of the elite is not "catholic" in any sense.

Most theologians who debate these matters are extremely committed Christians. They have much invested in the church, but may easily lose the perspective that church doors open wide to include the less committed as well.

Baptizing indiscriminately is no better, but all that is required for infant baptism and church membership is the pledge of Christian upbringing, not further proof of a response.

3) Requiring commitment raises a catechetical problem in explaining the nature of confirmation. As a sacrament of the Holy Spirit, confirmation is administered with the expression, "Be sealed with the Gift of the Holy Spirit." Adolescents who are required to attend confirmation programs and participate in activities which credit "service hours" to their scoresheets will fail to appreciate how confirmation is in any sense a "gift."[398] The impression that confirmation must be "earned" has caused many a teen to remark, "I don't want to be confirmed."[399] Such a statement would be incomprehensible to the Church Fathers who inaugurated the practice.

Catechists lack clear directives explaining how to judge who is ready for commitment. It's hard to imagine how the church could guide catechists in judging those already baptized about their readiness for membership.

A further catechetical problem is explaining why these "uncommitted" teens have been sharing communion. Most teens already participate in the Sunday eucharist. To require commitment for them to be confirmed is to claim that they need more commitment for confirmation than they do for eucharist.

4) Requiring commitment for both confirmation and membership sits squarely with the Methodist tradition; Catholic proponents of adolescent confirmation will find good company there. But such a position fails to recognize the full implications of infant baptism. Baptizing infants recognizes a different dynamic for those born into a Christian household. The practice assumes that birth into a Christian family will be birth into a Christian environment. The child of such a family has a "right" to be baptized, since Christianity is its faith environment. It's like being born an American, or into a particular family, culture, or neighborhood. All these groups have traditions and histories that become part of the newborn's life from its first day. There is no real "choice" involved in these formative elements: they are part of one's milieu. People sadly might withhold their commitment from those groups, but their membership endures.[400] Adolescent confirmation does not confer membership; it ritualizes maturity. Membership is accomplished long before teenage years. If teens need to celebrate maturity and commitment, and if the church offers them "initiation," it discredits their membership and withholds the rituals they need.

The Ritual Texts of Initiation

Several passages in the ritual texts cast doubt on the appropriateness of confirmation for teens.

The order of Christian initiation for adults devotes a section to the Christian Initiation of Children Who Have Reached Catechetical Age.[401] It pertains to "children, not baptized as infants, who have attained the use of reason and are of catechetical age."[402] These children celebrate confirmation as part of the rites of initiation, immediately following baptism and before first eucharist, usually at the Easter Vigil. The rite describes the capabilities of children:

Such children are capable of receiving and nurturing a

personal faith and of recognizing an obligation in conscience. But they cannot yet be treated as adults because, at this stage of their lives, they are dependent on their parents or guardians and are still strongly influenced by their companions and their social surroundings.[403]

The qualifications needed for children to be confirmed sound like those required for adolescents, yet the age set by the order is "catechetical age," when children have attained the use of reason. Further, the influence exerted by friends and social surroundings, which adolescent confirmation tries to help the candidate overcome, is regarded here as merely part of the catechetical environment. The goal of overcoming peer pressure is not a reason for delaying confirmation to teenage years. It is a challenge for catechesis to meet as children celebrate baptism and confirmation.

Further, when the time for the sacrament arrives, the suggested introduction of the celebrant says that confirmation will anoint the newly baptized "to be more like Christ, the Son of God." That is, it uses the same language used in adult initiation and in the delayed confirmation of children. But "to be more like Christ" does not refer to a maturity from time—confirmation follows immediately after baptism. Rather, it refers to a deepening of the Christian life through the gift of the Holy Spirit. One does not need physical maturity "to be more like Christ."

In an earlier passage describing the initiation of adults, the order speaks of their first sharing in the celebration of the eucharist:

> Finally in the celebration of the eucharist, as they take part for the first time and with full right, the newly baptized reach the culminating point in their Christian initiation. . . . When in communion they receive the body that was given for us and the blood that was shed, the neophytes are strengthened in the gifts they have already received and are given a foretaste of the eternal banquet.[404]

Here it is clear that eucharist, not confirmation is the culmination of initiation, and that eucharist in fact "strengthens"—a quality frequently attributed to confirmation.[405]

The order reiterates the same point when it describes the liturgy of the eucharist:

> Before saying "This is the Lamb of God," the celebrant may briefly remind the neophytes of the preeminence of the eucharist, which is the climax of their initiation and the center of the whole Christian life.[406]

Eucharist, not confirmation, is the "climax" and "center" of the Christian life.

Canonical Texts

As indicated earlier, the code of canon law assumes that confirmation will be celebrated after baptism and before eucharist. This is clear from the canons which list the sacraments of initiation and from the order in which the sacraments are treated in the "titles" or subdivisions of the whole book. A commentary on the code explains it this way:

> The canons of this title take for granted that confirmation, even in the case of those baptized as infants, will be received before participation in the Eucharist, in accord with the tradition of both sacraments. Where it is determined that confirmation should be postponed further for cause, as canon 891 allows under certain circumstances, this practice is treated in the canons as exceptional. Common as this practice is in many regions, it does invert the sequence of confirmation and Eucharist that is clearly indicated in the canons and in the liturgical books.[407]

Sequence and Meaning of Eucharist in Initiation

Church documents are not consistent about the sequence and meaning of eucharist in the sacraments of initiation. Ever since the catechumenate was restored after Vatican II, documents are careful to describe eucharist as the culmination of initiation. But there are places, as noted above,[408] where the texts imply that confirmation will follow eucharist.

Not so long ago the Congregation for Sacraments authored several appeals that confirmation precede first eucharist.[409] These requests have been disregarded in the movement toward adolescent confirmation.

The difficulty with the Eastern Rites is clear, since they see chrismation as a sacrament which prepares one for eucharist. This theology of initiation is lost in the west where confirmation is so frequently celebrated after first eucharist. The difference becomes more exaggerated when confirmation is delayed into teenage years for those who have received communion throughout their childhood.

Another difficulty surfaces when comparing delayed confirmation with the model of adult initiation. Among adults, no separate commitment is required for the sacraments of initiation. Commitment for one equals commitment for the others. Yet among children, delaying confirmation requires separate and deeper commitment as they mature.

Repeatability

Should confirmation become a repeatable sacrament? There are two schools of thought on this point, even within the field of those who support adolescent confirmation. Some say confirmation should retain its tradition as a once in a lifetime sacrament. Others say it now concerns an event (commitment) that happens over and over in life.

Does "commitment" happen once or many times? The sacraments of marriage and orders assume that once the commitment is made, it stays, but people are invited to renew their commitment when the opportunity arises. Assuming teens were already committed to the church to some degree as children, their confirmation might be seen as another level of commitment, or the kind of commitment ritual that need not be a once in a lifetime event.

If the event which adolescent confirmation ritualizes is a repeatable event, it is best to celebrate it with a repeatable ritual. Not to do so is to risk communicating to teens that adolescent commitment should resolve their commitment needs for a lifetime. That just isn't so. The experience of maturity and commitment happens many times in life. A ritual celebration for each would be appropriate. The church could either choose a celebration which can be repeated or redefine confirmation as a repeatable sacrament. But that's not so easy.

Confirmation enjoys a long history of irrepeatability because of its relationship to baptism. Confirmation, a seal on baptism, was a single celebration ratifying a single event. It is irrepeatable because of God's effective action; it recognizes the irrevocable presence of the Holy Spirit in the new members of the body of Christ. Once initiated, the Christian never needs initiation again. Thus confirmation's irrepeatability has to do with God's divine presence, not with an irrepeatable commitment on the part of the Christian. It has to do with incorporation in the body of Christ, not with one's imperfect decision to follow Christ, a decision which will be marred over and over by sin. This is why confirmation is accompanied with the words, "Be sealed with the Gift of the Holy Spirit," instead of, "Congratulations on your commitment." Confirmation is about what God does, not about what candidates do. The irrepeatability of confirmation argues for its celebration in proximity with baptism.

From the point of view of sacramental and liturgical history, the use of chrism at confirmation becomes problematic if confirmation were to become a repeatable celebration. Chrism is the oil used in the three non-repeatable sacraments in the church: baptism, confirmation, and orders. The reason is that chrism represents the presence of the Holy Spirit in the anointing of God's people, a presence which is permanent and unchanging. If a repeatable confirmation were to re-anoint with chrism, it would weaken the power of that symbol in its other uses.

Canonically, of course, the case is closed. Confirmation impresses a character[410] and may be received only by those who have not been confirmed.[411] The Oriental code says it most openly: "The sacraments of baptism, chrismation of holy chrism, and holy order, cannot be repeated."[412]

A related matter is the "sacramental character," traditionally explained in the church as an effect of the same three non-repeatable sacraments. The metaphor of "impressing a character on the soul" limps, but the point remains: There are certain sacraments which make a lifetime change in a person. Confirmation is one of them, since it celebrates the coming of the Holy Spirit on the baptized. If it becomes a repeatable celebration, it will weaken the image of the Spirit's irrevocable coming.

The church has a long history of theology surrounding the sacramental character, its meaning in the sacraments, and in the life of the one anointed. Changing the practice of confirmation is potentially a larger question than one of age; it concerns the very philosophy of how sacraments work.

Origins

Attempts to trace the origins of confirmation to Scripture are troublesome to all. No matter what model one chooses, it's hard to document it in the Bible. Tempting as it is to turn to Acts 8 and 19 for irrefutable evidence, to do so is to read a much later practice into a very early record. Simply put, to call Acts 8 and 19 confirmation is an anachronism.

Besides, Acts 10, 44–48 presents another story which adds to the dilemma: The Holy Spirit falls upon some Gentiles "as at (Pentecost)" (Acts 11, 15) *before* they are baptized at all! The evidence from Acts is sparse and inconsistent.

Even if one were to allow that the imposition of hands in Acts 8 and 19 demonstrates part of the initiation rites for two communities of the apostolic church, it is dangerous to universalize those texts: Just because there are two records is no reason to indicate this was the customary practice. Besides, there is absolutely no biblical evidence for separating the rites of baptism and imposition of hands by seventeen years, or for celebrating a "commitment" of those who had already been baptized. Claims that the anointing in confirmation dates to apostolic times are completely unsupportable.[413]

Identifying the origins of confirmation is an important quest because the church still relies on ancient texts for a ceremony that accompanies universal human needs—the need to belong, the need for redemption. The real question is to which origins does one turn? Confirmation was several different rites even in the early church: initiation, reconciliation, and belonging to the universal church. The difficulty in clearing up the many models of confirmation found in the church today is that they stem from a variety of models already in place fifteen hundred years ago. It's hard to rectify that much history.

To understand the problem of origins it might be helpful to imagine another scenario. Suppose not initiation, but marriage split into separate rites. Imagine that in a country where priests are scarce, an episcopal conference asked permission for catechists to act as witnesses for marriage, but the ring ceremony would be reserved for a priest. When a priest visited the parish, he would bless the rings and invite the couple to exchange them as a sign of their love. Now suppose that twenty years later this situation continued, but the catechists began reinterpreting the symbols: The exchange of vows before the catechist indicated the couple's understanding of the marriage they are beginning, but after some years of experimenting to see if this relationship really is the one they wish to keep, the ring ceremony became the ceremony of commitment. All this time, those couples who wed in parishes where a priest was present celebrated both rituals in the same ceremony. Are there two different sacraments going on here? What are the implications for the exchange of vows?

If adolescent confirmation is to be recognized as a true evolution in history, it will help to know if it remains true to its roots— true enough to carry the name "confirmation." It is "initiation" only by redefining the term. It serves as a symbol of unity in the diocesan church only when the bishop is present. And that is not always the case. In fact, the minister is not so important an issue at all. Adolescent confirmation concerns the individual's faith, not the bishop's presence. Hence, its connection to confirmation's roots are difficult to see.

Interest in adolescent confirmation arose at the same time in church history that the catechumenate was revived. Perhaps seeing the advantages of committed adults created a new vision of church. Not a few who were baptized in infancy have looked longingly on the newly baptized at the Easter Vigil, wishing they could have had a ritual so powerful in their adult lives. Adolescent confirmation may be trying to fill a loss that Catholics baptized in infancy feel, now that they can witness the fullness of the rites of initiation for adults.

The question remains, how faithful is adolescent confirmation to the traditional sacrament whose name it borrows? Can sacraments change? If so, how far, before they evolve into a new species altogether?

The Baby in Solomon's Court

Confirmation deserves our grief. It is like the baby in King Solomon's court.[414] Two women claimed the child. To determine who was its real mother, Solomon ordered the baby cut in two. Then he listened for which woman wailed, and rescued the baby for her. Throughout the centuries, many different schools and traditions have claimed to be the true mother of confirmation, and the church, imitating Solomon, has let them all have their say. Tragically, the result is unlike Solomon's: the mothers are tearing the baby apart. Not only does the church suffer the infighting of its own theologians, but the sacrament itself is rendered confusing and meaningless by its overuse, overscrutiny, and misapplication.

Around every boxing match stands a ring. The fight takes place within the ropes, never outside. The ropes around the fight for confirmation are the tradition in the church that there are seven sacraments. Only seven. The models of confirmation all vie for the sacramental prize. The church cannot admit that adolescent confirmation is a different sacrament from initiatory sealing without breaking the ropes.

How many sacraments are there? Seven? Two? Or are there too many to count? If there were no ropes, there would be no boxing match.

7

Confirmation in Danger of Death

Introduction

A dying Catholic who has never been confirmed has immediate access to the sacrament through any priest. This model of confirmation is celebrated less frequently than the others. Most Catholics either were confirmed earlier in life or die before they take the opportunity.

The order of confirmation devotes a separate chapter to confirmation of a person in danger of death.[415] It states,

> It is of the greatest importance that the initiation of every baptized Christian be completed by the sacraments of confirmation and the eucharist.[416]

The document introducing the sacrament of the anointing of the sick says,

> It is highly appropriate that the initiation of every baptized Christian be completed by the sacraments of confirmation and the eucharist.[417]

Eligible is "the sick person in danger of death who has reached the age of reason," and the child who has not yet reached the age of reason "in accord with the same principles and norms as for baptism."[418] That is, if parents, guardians, and/or godparents speak on behalf of the child, the child who is eligible for infant baptism when healthy may also be confirmed in danger of death.

Confirmation should be preceded by whatever catechesis is "necessary and possible,"[419] and followed by communion, given as viaticum. Viaticum is the last sacrament of Christian life, celebrated when death is close.[420]

By treating confirmation in this context, the order indicates yet another meaning and occasion for the sacrament: it forms part of the church's pastoral care for the dying.

The Rite

The rite takes place in one of three different forms, differing only in length and content.

If the dying person is capable of it, the **whole** order of confirmation may be followed, just as it is for healthy children or adolescents.[421]

An **abbreviated** form suits cases of urgent necessity. This form includes only two parts: the laying on of hands with the prayer for the Holy Spirit, and the anointing with chrism and the formula, "N., be sealed with the Gift of the Holy Spirit."[422]

In extreme necessity the rite may be abbreviated further: The second part—the **formula** alone—may be given with the anointing of chrism.[423]

The order of confirmation suggests that confirmation in danger of death and anointing of the sick should not be celebrated in the same rite.[424] No reason is given. It might appear that since the anointing of the sick prays for healing it could be at cross-purposes with confirmation when death is near. However, anointing may be administered even with viaticum, when death is presumed to be near. Only in the *Pastoral Care of the Sick* does one find this explanation:

> It is preferable not to celebrate the sacrament of confirmation and the sacrament of the anointing of the sick in a continuous rite. The two anointings can cause some confusion between the two sacraments. However, if the dying person has not

been confirmed this sacrament may be celebrated immediately before the blessing of the oil of the sick. In this case, the imposition of hands which is part of the liturgy of anointing is omitted.[425]

The fear of confusion expressed here supports the assumption that this model of confirmation forms part of pastoral care for the dying. In fact, confirmation should replace the anointing of the sick for those dying unconfirmed. In rare cases when both sacraments are administrated together (with two different oils), only one imposition of hands suffices, and it belongs with confirmation.

Comments

Some noteworthy aspects of the rite include the minister, the catechesis, and the ease of celebration.

The minister may be any priest. The code of canon law grants this permission.[426] This permission demonstrates both the church's concern for the dying person and the church's respect for confirmation: It seeks to make the sacrament more accessible.

If the dying person has never been baptized, the order specifies what action to take according to a hierarchy of ministers: If no bishop is available, a priest may celebrate all the rites. If no priest is available, a deacon may celebrate all rites except confirmation; he may, however, offer the post-baptismal anointing with chrism on the crown of the head. If no deacon is available, a lay eucharistic minister may baptize and bring viaticum. If no lay eucharistic minister is available, anyone may baptize.[427]

The hierarchy of ministers shows also a hierarchy of sacraments: The church is most desirous that the unbaptized be baptized; it matters less that they be confirmed.

Catechesis for confirmation is encouraged, even in danger of death, but as it is "necessary and possible." This instruction shows the importance of catechesis for those who have reached the age of reason. However, by allowing confirmation to children below the age of reason on the same grounds as infant baptism, the order indicates that in this extreme case catechesis is no more required for confirmation than it is for infant baptism. This stresses the nature of confirmation as an unearned gift of the Spirit, and its distinction from sacraments like marriage and holy orders, which both require catechesis under absolutely all circumstances.

The ease with which the sacrament is given is also striking. The church clearly senses some urgency in this case. It desires to remove obstacles to the celebration of confirmation. Confirmation is indeed "of the greatest importance" and "highly appropriate" for all Christians. This is so true that the church offers it effortlessly to the dying.

Concerns

Even such a pastoral response to the dying raises some concerns about how this practice affects the meaning of confirmation.

The church calls confirmation a sacrament of initiation. The term is meaningless for the dying. Here confirmation is a sacrament like viaticum, celebrated under special circumstances for those near death. It marks the end of the Christian journey, not its beginning.

The ease with which confirmation is offered for the dying seems to betray an apology from the church. There was no hint of a final chance for confirmation in one canon:

> The faithful are obliged to receive this sacrament at the appropriate time; their parents and shepherds of souls, especially pastors, are to see to it that the faithful are properly instructed to receive it and approach the sacrament at the appropriate time.[428]

The order of confirmation contains a similar worry:

> (In the case of delaying confirmation to a more mature age) the necessary precautions should be taken so that children will be confirmed at the proper time, even before the use of reason, where there is danger of death or other serious difficulty. They should not be deprived of the benefit of this sacrament.[429]

The order of funerals presumes that the deceased Christian has celebrated all three sacraments of initiation. Intercessions for the rite of committal include the following:

> Our brother/sister was washed in baptism and anointed with the Holy Spirit; give him/her fellowship with all your saints.

> He/she was nourished with your body and blood; grant him/her a place at the table in your heavenly kingdom.[430]

Offering confirmation at time of death indicates the church's hope that everyone be confirmed, and its regret that this has not happened. A special rite for those in danger of death admits that something is wrong in the confirmation policy. It is a sacrament "of the greatest importance," yet one which many are allowed to miss. Once confirmation was deferred from baptism, the church opened the possibility that some Christians will never celebrate it at all.

Sadly, this possibility has existed all through history. Bishops all over the western world and in every age have lamented that many of those baptized have not been confirmed. Every diocese today will admit the same. Sacramental records typically show twice as many baptisms as confirmations each year. The popularity of adolescent confirmation has not stopped this trend. In spite of the best efforts at catechesis and pastoral care at every stage of life's journey, in spite of the belief that confirmation is one of the greatest gifts imaginable, the gift of the Holy Spirit—the church has so restricted its celebration that, in spite of the simple provisions for confirmation in danger of death, many will never be confirmed.

Conclusion

Confirmation is a sacrament which has found too many theologies. It originated from several sources, and its strains stay mixed. Its origins remain sketchy, and their ambiguity has permitted a broad range of development.

Now, confirmation has come to bear too much. It staggers under the weight of its complex history and struggles to meet the needs of the modern age where the number of Christians is huge, the press of secular religion is strong, the need for committed Christians is large, and the demands on the Holy Spirit are desperate.

To sort out the confusion over confirmation it will help to think of three different models from the early church: The first stood within the baptismal rites of initiation. Here, the imposition of hands and/or anointing accompanied a catechumen's initiation into the church. The second marked the reconciliation of heretics. In this case an imposition of hands and/or anointing symbolized the restoration of membership to the orthodox church. The third model deferred the bishop's anointing to a time some years after the presbyter's baptism. All these rites included the same dominant gestures: anointing with chrism and some form of imposing hands.

The seven models of confirmation discussed above can trace their origins to these three sources. Adult initiation and the Eastern Rites come from the initiation tradition. Catholic initiation resembles the rites of reconciling heretics. The Protestant-Anglican celebrations and the confirmation of children and adolescents all derive from the rite deferred from baptism. Confirmation for the dying is an anomaly that tries finally to catch those whom the other forms missed.

For the Catholic Church to untangle confirmation will require a solution similar to that chosen by many Protestant-Anglican Churches: to acknowledge that what we call "confirmation" actually represents several different phenomena. Our liturgies tell us we have three separate needs: the need to emphasize the gift of the Spirit in the rites of initiation, the need to mark a transfer of membership from another Christian church into the Catholic Church, and the need for children baptized in infancy to affirm their baptism and strengthen their faith and commitment.

Why can't they all be called confirmation? That is the case now, and the solution pleases no one. A rite of initiation is not the same as a rite of transfer or of commitment. Rites of transfer only heighten the intolerable situation of Christian disunity. And the need to recommit and celebrate the strengthening of faith is a need best ritualized by a repeatable celebration.

If we could start all over and imagine a day when our ancestors devised these rituals, if we could say, "We need a rite of initiation, a rite of transfer, and a rite of maturity," would we choose the *same* rite and the *same* name for all three events? Of course not, yet this is the burden we have laid on the sacrament of confirmation.

If we could separate the rituals, we could also simplify our imagery. Initiation would celebrate the "gift" of the Spirit; transfer of membership the "seal"; and the rite of Christian maturity could be the Spirit's "strengthening."

Catechesis would become more direct. Confirmation in initiation would share baptismal catechesis. Transfer of membership would require "communion-specific" catechesis. And the rite of Christian maturity could presuppose lectionary catechesis, in which the candidates are steeped more deeply in the tradition they have shared in all their lives.

We can only hope that the need for a rite of transferring membership will become minimized. Progress in the ecumenical movement should help us move toward a single eucharistic table for all Christian families. This would reduce the need for a separate rite of "Reception of Baptized Christians into the Full Communion of the Catholic Church"[431] and purify the purpose of confirmation.

Current pastoral practice sadly initiates such candidates in much the same way as catechumens. The two groups are catechized together, and pass through either the same rituals or ponderous adaptations which struggle to challenge the non-baptized without offending non-Catholic Christians. Frequently, candidates are disappointed that they cannot be baptized like catechumens, that they should not sign the book of the elect like catechumens, that they are not called to scrutinies like catechumens, that they are not anointed with the oil of catechumens like catechumens. This disappointment often belies poorly trained catechists who revere liturgical innovation more than the baptism of other Christian churches. By making candidates imitate the path of catechumens we have too often made it too difficult for Christians who share one baptism to share one eucharistic table. The ecumenical movement longs for the day when the rites which prepare baptized Christians for full communion will be ripped from our books, and the catechumenate now so freely adapted for the *baptized* may become again the proper province of the unbaptized.

When the disciples warned Jesus that some who were not of their company were exorcising demons in his name they expected him to put a stop to it.[432] Jesus tolerated strange exorcists with the simplest of aphorisms: "If they're not against us, they're for us." The church tolerates baptisms. Is it too much to ask that we tolerate confirmations as well? Our churches are irresponsibly dawdling toward a common table.

From there the main question would be, "Which rite should we call confirmation?" Many Protestant-Anglican Churches have opted for the maturity rite. This has some historical footing, since the name "confirmation" was not common until after the anointing with chrism separated from baptism. What has no historical footing is making this a repeatable rite. It's true that in Orthodoxy, chrismation is repeatable in rare instances, but chrismation befits either the rites of initiation or the transfer of membership, not a rite of maturity.

What is unnecessary to repeat about this sacrament is the gift of the Holy Spirit. Once the Spirit comes it is here to stay. That coming is most obviously ritualized in initiation: Once a member, always a member. So an irrepeatable rite at initiation might remain the logical historical successor to what we've called "confirmation" in initiation, but a later repeatable maturity ritual could be a logical evolution in the development of confirmation as maturity rite. It matters little which one wins the name; it matters a great deal that these rites be separated by title and intent.

To do nothing is to place the sacrament of confirmation at great risk. The richness of its meaning has already been rendered obscure to most members of the church. The fights between liturgists and catechists, historians and romantics, Catholics and Orthodox, Protestants and Catholics embarrass the body of Christ over a matter which should rather celebrate our principle of unity: the gift of God's Holy Spirit. Our intransigence is tearing confirmation apart, rendering it ridiculous. In initiation, it pales in significance before baptism and eucharist. In adolescence, its hype mocks baptismal initiation. Many young people who have claimed it as a rite of "commitment" have turned it into a rite of exit from the church, the goodbye sacrament. And many more will never celebrate confirmation at all. To do nothing about confirmation is to confuse its meaning, since it exists under so many forms. To do nothing is to obscure the paschal mystery, since the many different occasions for the sacrament destroy its proximity to baptism, where it expresses the link between the mission of the Son and the outpouring of the Spirit. To do nothing is to encumber the Holy Spirit; this sacrament is supposed to symbolize the Spirit's nature, mission, and gift, but it rather symbolizes how poorly we comprehend and explain the Spirit's presence.

To resolve the confirmation dilemma will not only require unanimity within the Catholic Church, it will also demand huge ecumenical overtures. Are we prepared for these questions: What is a sacrament? How many are there? Does the gift of the Spirit come in baptism? If not, why do we defer this gift, this grace, this help, this miracle—why do we defer it at all? Why should infants be denied the gift of the Spirit? Further, why should they be denied the eucharist? Are they not members of the body of Christ? Does the gift of the Holy Spirit come in Protestant baptism? Does commitment happen once in life? Is Orthodox chrismation the same as Catholic confirmation? Until we are prepared for these matters we will doom ourselves to petty, endless, unresolvable cocktail-hour debates over what confirmation means and how old its candidates should be. Participants retreat from such conversations to find like-minded advocates, like addicts in search of twelve-step support groups.

In some ways confirmation is an insignificant ceremony, a decorative span which straddles the pillars of baptism and eucharist. In other ways it is an explosive device that our churches are content to let tick and fearful to dismantle. And while the baby screams amidst its mothers, Solomon ponders what to do.

Appendix I

Synopsis of Baptism and Confirmation Rites

Key to the Synopsis

1 Consecration of chrism
2 Rites preparatory to baptism
3 Baptismal rites
4 Rites preparatory to confirmation or postbaptismal rites
5 Imposition of hands and/or prayer for the Holy Spirit
6 Anointing with chrism or oil
7 Concluding rites

A. Roman Catholic Church
Rite of Christian Initiation of Adults[433]

(Mass of Chrism, held in each diocese once a year, precedes this celebration. At that Mass, the bishop consecrates chrism for the initiation rites.)

1

CELEBRATION OF BAPTISM

Presentation of the Candidates

Invitation to Prayer

Litany of the Saints

Prayer over the Water

Profession of Faith

2

Baptism

3

Explanatory Rites

4

CELEBRATION OF CONFIRMATION

If the bishop is not present, the priest who conferred baptism confirms.

INVITATION

The celebrant first speaks briefly to the newly baptized in these or similar words.

My dear newly baptized, born again in Christ by baptism, you have become members of Christ and of his priestly people. Now you are to share in the outpouring of the Holy Spirit among us, the Spirit sent by the Lord upon his apostles at Pentecost and given by them and their successors to the baptized.

The promised strength of the Holy Spirit, which you are to receive, will make you more like Christ and help you to be witnesses to his suffering, death, and resurrection. It will strengthen you to be active members of the Church and to build up the Body of Christ in faith and love.

With hands joined, the celebrant next addresses the people:

My dear friends, let us pray to God our Father, that he will pour out the Holy Spirit on these newly baptized to strengthen them with his gifts and anoint them to be more like Christ, the Son of God.

All pray briefly in silence.

5

B. Roman Catholic Church
Rite of Baptism for Children[434]
Rite of Confirmation[435]

(Mass of Chrism, held in each diocese once a year, precedes this celebration. At that Mass, the bishop consecrates chrism for the initiation rites.)

1

RITE OF BAPTISM FOR CHILDREN

RECEPTION OF THE CHILDREN

CELEBRATION OF GOD'S WORD

CELEBRATION OF THE SACRAMENT

Blessing and Invocation of God over Baptismal Water

Renunciation of Sin and Profession of Faith

2

Baptism

Anointing with Chrism

Then the celebrant says:

God the Father of our Lord Jesus Christ has freed you from sin, given you a new birth by water and the Holy Spirit, and welcomed you into his holy people. He now anoints you with the chrism of salvation. As Christ was anointed Priest, Prophet, and King, so may you live always as members of his body, sharing everlasting life.
All: Amen.

Next, the celebrant anoints each child on the crown of the head with chrism, in silence.

Conclusion of the Rite

3

RITE OF CONFIRMATION

PRESENTATION OF THE CANDIDATES
[A minister presents the candidates by name. Children are led to the sanctuary by a sponsor or parent.]

HOMILY OR INSTRUCTION

RENEWAL OF BAPTISMAL PROMISES

4

THE LAYING ON OF HANDS

[The Bishop says,]
My dear friends:
in baptism God our Father gave the new birth of eternal life
to his chosen sons and daughters.
Let us pray to our Father
that he will pour out the Holy Spirit
to strengthen his sons and daughters with his gifts
and anoint them to be more like Christ the Son of God.

All pray in silence for a short time.

The bishop and the priests who will minister the sacrament with him lay hands upon all the candidates (by extending their hands over them). The bishop alone sings or says:

All-powerful God, Father of our Lord Jesus Christ,
by water and the Holy Spirit
you freed your sons and daughters from sin
and gave them new life.
Send your Holy Spirit upon them
to be their Helper and Guide.
Give them the spirit of wisdom and understanding,
the spirit of right judgment and courage,
the spirit of knowledge and reverence.
Fill them with the spirit of wonder and awe in your presence.
We ask this through Christ our Lord.

R. Amen.

THE ANOINTING WITH CHRISM

[The parent or sponsor places his or her right hand on the shoulder of the one to be confirmed and gives the candidate's name to the bishop.]

The bishop dips his right thumb in the chrism and makes the sign of the cross on the forehead of the one to be confirmed, as he says:

N., be sealed with the Gift of the Holy Spirit.
The newly confirmed responds: Amen.

The bishop says:
Peace be with you.
The newly confirmed responds: And also with you.

[During the anointing a song may be sung.]

The celebrant holds his hands outstretched over the entire group of those to be confirmed and says the following prayer.

All-powerful God, Father of our Lord Jesus Christ,
by water and the Holy Spirit
you freed your sons and daughters from sin
and gave them new life.
Send your Holy Spirit upon them
to be their helper and guide.
Give them the spirit of wisdom and understanding,
the spirit of right judgment and courage,
the spirit of knowledge and reverence.
Fill them with the spirit of wonder and awe in your presence.
We ask this through Christ our Lord.
R. Amen.

ANOINTING WITH CHRISM

Either or both godparents place the right hand on the shoulder of the candidate and either a godparent or the candidate gives the candidate's name to the minister of the sacrament. During the conferral of the sacrament a suitable song may be sung.

The minister of the sacrament dips his right thumb in the chrism and makes the sign of the cross on the forehead of the one to be confirmed as he says:

N., be sealed with the Gift of the Holy Spirit.
Newly confirmed:
Amen.

The minister of the sacrament adds:
Peace be with you.
Newly confirmed:
And also with you.

1 Consecration of chrism 2 Rites preparatory to baptism 3 Baptismal rites 4 Rites preparatory to confirmation or post-baptismal rites 5 Imposition of hands and/or prayer for the Holy Spirit 6 Anointing with chrism or oil 7 Concluding rites

D. The Lutheran Church—Missouri Synod
Holy Baptism[438]
Confirmation[439]

HOLY BAPTISM

(Gathering of the group)

The minister lays his hand upon the head of the child. The congregation joins in praying:

Our Father. . . .

(Renunciation and Profession)

(Baptism)

The minister lays his hand upon the one baptized and gives this blessing:

Almighty God, the Father of our Lord Jesus Christ, who has given you the new birth of water and of the Spirit and has forgiven you all your sins, strengthen you with his grace to life everlasting. Peace be with you.

(Conclusion)

CONFIRMATION

After a hymn of invocation of the Holy Spirit has been sung, the catechumens gather before the altar, and the minister addresses them. . . .

(PRESENTATION). . . .

(EXAMINATION, CONFESSION OF FAITH). . . .

2

3

4

C. Evangelical Lutheran Church in America
Holy Baptism[436]
Affirmation of Baptism[437]

HOLY BAPTISM

(Presentation of candidates)

(Renunciation and Profession)

(Baptism)

Those who have been baptized kneel. Sponsors or parents holding young children stand. The minister lays both hands on the head of each of the baptized and prays for the Holy Spirit:

God, the Father of our Lord Jesus Christ, we give you thanks for freeing your sons and daughters from the power of sin and for raising them up to a new life through this holy sacrament. Pour your Holy Spirit upon name : the spirit of wisdom and understanding, the spirit of counsel and might, the spirit of knowledge and the fear of the Lord, the spirit of joy in your presence.

Amen.

The minister marks the sign of the cross on the forehead of each of the baptized. Oil prepared for this purpose may be used. As the sign of the cross is made, the minister says:

name , child of God, you have been sealed by the Holy Spirit and marked with the cross of Christ forever.

The sponsor of the baptized responds: "Amen."

(Conclusion)

2

3

5

6

The catechumens, in turn, give their right hand and kneel. The minister lays his hands upon the head of each one and gives the following blessing. A confirmation text is then given to each.

name___, God, the Father of our Lord Jesus Christ, give you his Holy Spirit, the Spirit of wisdom and knowledge, of grace and prayer, of power and strength, of sanctification and the fear of God.

After all catechumens have received the blessing and text of Scripture, the minister says:

Upon this your profession and promise I invite and welcome you, as members of the Evangelical Lutheran Church and of this congregation, to share with us in all the gifts our Lord has for his Church and to live them out continually in his worship and service.

The minister invites the congregation to pray for the newly confirmed.

Let us pray for the newly confirmed.

Lord God, heavenly Father, we thank and praise you for your great goodness in bringing these your sons and daughters to the knowledge of your Son, our Savior, Jesus Christ, and enabling them both with the heart to believe and with the mouth to confess his saving name. Grant that, bringing forth the fruits of faith, they may continue steadfast and victorious to the day when all who have fought the good fight of faith shall receive the crown of righteousness; through Jesus Christ, your Son, our Lord, who lives and reigns with you and the Holy Spirit, one God, now and forever.

Amen.

The minister dismisses the newly confirmed with a blessing.

1 Consecration of chrism   2 Rites preparatory to baptism   3 Baptismal rites   4 Rites preparatory to confirmation or post-baptismal rites   5 Imposition of hands and/or prayer for the Holy Spirit   6 Anointing with chrism or oil   7 Concluding rites

---

AFFIRMATION OF BAPTISM

A hymn is sung as the candidates gather before the congregation.

CONFIRMATION
(Presentation)
The candidates' names are read.

RECEPTION INTO MEMBERSHIP.....

RESTORATION TO MEMBERSHIP.....

(PROFESSION OF FAITH)

(PRAYERS).....
The minister says:
Gracious Lord, through water and the Spirit you have made these men and women your own. You forgave them all their sins and brought them to newness of life. Continue to strengthen them with the Holy Spirit, and daily increase in them your gifts of grace: the spirit of wisdom and understanding, the spirit of counsel and might, the spirit of knowledge and the fear of the Lord, the spirit of joy in your presence; through Jesus Christ, your Son, our Lord.

Amen.

FOR CONFIRMATION ONLY
The presiding minister lays both hands on the head of each person:
Father in heaven, for Jesus' sake, stir up in name the gift of your Holy Spirit; confirm his/her faith, guide his/her life, empower him/her in his/her serving, give him/her patience in suffering, and bring him/her to everlasting life.

Each person answers: ''Amen.''

They stand. The presiding minister exchanges the peace with each of them. They exchange the peace with one another and other members of the congregation:

Peace be with you.

E. The Presbyterian Church (U.S.A.)
An Order for Holy Baptism[440]

AN ORDER FOR HOLY BAPTISM

2   Presentation

Renunciation and Affirmation

Thanksgiving over the Water

3   The Act of Baptizing

The Blessing (and Anointing)

The MINISTER lays hands on the head of the person baptized while saying:

O Lord, uphold _____ by your Holy Spirit.
Give *(him, her)* the spirit of wisdom and understanding,
the spirit of counsel and might,
the spirit of knowledge and the fear of the Lord,
the spirit of joy in your presence,
both now and forever.

5   **Amen.**

Or

Defend, O Lord, your servant _____
with your heavenly grace,
that *(he, she)* may continue yours forever,
and daily increase in your Holy Spirit more and more,
until *(he, she)* comes to your everlasting kingdom.

F. The Presbyterian Church (U.S.A.)
Public Profession of Faith[441]

4

PRESENTATION
A hymn, psalm, spiritual, or other suitable music may be sung. . . .

RENUNCIATION AND AFFIRMATION. . . .

THE BLESSING (AND ANOINTING)

The CANDIDATES kneel.

The MINISTER in turn lays both hands upon the head of each candidate while offering the following prayer. The sign of the cross may be marked on the forehead of the candidate, using oil prepared for this purpose:

O Lord, uphold _____ by your Holy Spirit.
Daily increase in *(him, her)* your gifts of grace:
the spirit of wisdom and understanding,
the spirit of counsel and might,
the spirit of knowledge and the fear of the Lord,
the spirit of joy in your presence,
both now and forever.

The CANDIDATE answers:

Amen.

Or

Defend, O Lord, your servant _____
with your heavenly grace,
that *(he, she)* may continue yours forever,
and daily increase in your Holy Spirit more and more,
until *(he, she)* comes to your everlasting kingdom.

The CANDIDATE answers:

Amen.

5 & 6

As the MINISTER says these words, the sign of the cross may be marked on the forehead of the person baptized, using oil prepared for this purpose:

____, child of the covenant,
you have been sealed by the Holy Spirit in baptism,
and marked as Christ's own forever.

Amen.

Or

____, child of God,
you have been sealed by the Holy Spirit in baptism,
and grafted into Christ forever.

Amen.

Welcome

1 Consecration of chrism 2 Rites preparatory to baptism 3 Baptismal rites 4 Rites preparatory to confirmation or post-baptismal rites 5 Imposition of hands and/or prayer for the Holy Spirit 6 Anointing with chrism or oil 7 Concluding rites

---

After each candidate has received the laying on of hands, the MINISTER prays:

Ever-living God,
guard these your servants with your protecting hand,
and let your Holy Spirit be with *them* forever.
Lead *them* to know and obey your Word
that *they* may serve you in this life
and dwell with you in the life to come;
through Jesus Christ our Lord.

Amen.

An appropriate gift may be given to each person. Such gifts might include a cross or a book of prayers.

The MINISTER and ELDER exchange the peace with those who have renewed their baptism. They may exchange the peace with each other and members of the congregation.

The peace of Christ be with you.

And also with you.

H. The Episcopal Church
Confirmation with Forms for Reception and for Reaffirmation of Baptismal Vows[443]

A hymn, psalm, or anthem may be sung.

PRESENTATION AND EXAMINATION OF THE CANDIDATES . . . .

THE BAPTISMAL COVENANT (profession of faith) . . . .

Prayers for the Candidates. . . .

The Bishop says

Almighty God, we thank you that by the death and resurrection of your Son Jesus Christ you have overcome sin and brought us to yourself, and that by the sealing of your Holy Spirit you have bound us to your service. Renew in *these* your *servants* the covenant you made with *them* at *their* Baptism. Send *them* forth in the power of that Spirit to perform the service you set before *them*; through Jesus Christ your Son our Lord, who lives and reigns with you and the Holy Spirit, one God, now and for ever. *Amen.*

For Confirmation

The Bishop lays hands upon each one and says

Strengthen, O Lord, your servant *N.* with your Holy Spirit; empower *him* for your service; and sustain *him* all the days of *his* life. *Amen.*

or this

Defend, O Lord, your servant *N.* with your heavenly grace, that *he* may continue yours for ever, and daily increase in your holy Spirit more and more, until *he* comes to your everlasting kingdom. *Amen.*

G. The Episcopal Church
Holy Baptism[442]

HOLY BAPTISM

(Introductory Rites)

Presentation and Examination of the Candidates

The Baptismal Covenant (Creed)

Thanksgiving over the Water

Consecration of the Chrism

The Bishop may then consecrate the oil of Chrism, placing a hand on the vessel of oil, and saying

Eternal Father, whose blessed Son was anointed by the Holy Spirit to be the Savior and servant of all, we pray you to consecrate this oil, that those who are sealed with it may share in the royal priesthood of Jesus Christ; who lives and reigns with you and the Holy Spirit, for ever and ever. *Amen.*

The Baptism

When this action has been completed for all candidates, the Bishop or Priest, at a place in full sight of the congregation, prays over them, saying

Let us pray.

Heavenly Father, we thank you that by water and the Holy Spirit you have bestowed upon *these* your *servants* the forgiveness of sin, and have raised *them* to the new life of grace. Sustain *them*, O Lord, in your Holy Spirit. Give *them* an inquiring and discerning heart, the courage to will and to persevere, a spirit to know and to love you, and the gift of joy and wonder in all your works. *Amen.*

. . . marking on the forehead the sign of the cross (using Chrism if desired) and saying to each one

N., you are sealed by the Holy Spirit in Baptism and marked as Christ's own for ever. Amen.

Or this action may be done immediately after the administration of the water and before the preceding prayer.

(Welcome)

At Confirmation, Reception, or Reaffirmation

The Bishop says to the congregation

Let us now pray for *these persons* who *have* renewed *their* commitment to Christ.

Silence may be kept.

Then the Bishop says

Almighty God, we thank you that by the death and resurrection of your Son Jesus Christ you have overcome sin and brought us to yourself, and that by the sealing of your Holy Spirit you have bound us to your service. Renew in *these* your *servants* the covenant you made with *them* at *their* Baptism. Send *them* forth in the power of that Spirit to perform the service you set before *them*; through Jesus Christ your Son our Lord, who lives and reigns with you and the Holy Spirit, one God, now and forever. Amen.

For Confirmation

The Bishop lays hands upon each one and says

Strengthen, O Lord, your servant N. with your Holy Spirit; empower *him* for your service; and sustain *him* all the days of *his* life. Amen.

or this

Defend, O Lord, your servant N. with your heavenly grace, that *he* may continue yours for ever, and daily increase in your Holy Spirit more and more, until *he* comes to your everlasting kingdom. Amen.

Reception

Reaffirmation

Reaffirmation. . . .

The Peace is then exchanged

Bishop The peace of the Lord be always with you.
People And also with you. . . .

The Bishop may consecrate oil of Chrism for use at Baptism } 1

1 Consecration of chrism   2 Rites preparatory to baptism   3 Baptismal rites   4 Rites preparatory to confirmation or post-baptismal rites   5 Imposition of hands and/or prayer for the Holy Spirit   6 Anointing with chrism or oil   7 Concluding rites

I. The United Methodist Church
The Baptismal Covenant I⁴⁴⁴

INTRODUCTION TO THE SERVICE
An appropriate hymn of baptism or confirmation may be sung.

The pastor makes the following statement to the congregation:
Brothers and sisters in Christ:
Through the Sacrament of Baptism
   we are initiated into Christ's holy church.
We are incorporated into God's mighty acts of salvation
   and given new birth through water and the Spirit.
All this is God's gift, offered to us without price.

If there are confirmations or reaffirmations, the pastor continues:
Through confirmation,
   and through the reaffirmation of our faith,
   we renew the covenant declared at our baptism,
   acknowledge what God is doing for us,
   and affirm our commitment to Christ's holy church.

PRESENTATION OF CANDIDATES
A representative of the congregation presents the candidates with the appropriate statements:
I present *Name(s)* for baptism.
I present *Name(s)* for confirmation.
I present *Name(s)* to reaffirm *their* faith.
I present *Name(s)* who come(s) to this congregation from the _____ Church.

RENUNCIATION OF SIN AND PROFESSION OF FAITH
The pastor addresses parents or other sponsors and those candidates who can answer for themselves. . . .

THANKSGIVING OVER THE WATER. . . .

As the pastor, and others if desired, place hands on the head of each person being confirmed or reaffirming faith, the pastor says to each:

Name, the Holy Spirit work within you,
that having been born through water and the Spirit,
you may live as a faithful disciple of Jesus Christ.

All respond:

Amen. . . .

RECEPTION INTO THE UNITED METHODIST CHURCH. . . .

RECEPTION INTO THE LOCAL CONGREGATION. . . .

COMMENDATION AND WELCOME

The pastor addresses the congregation:
Members of the household of God,
I commend *these persons* to your love and care.
Do all in your power to increase *their* faith,
confirm *their* hope, and perfect *them* in love.

The congregation responds:

**We give thanks for all that God has already given you
   and we welcome you in Christian love.
As members together with you
   in the body of Christ
   and in this congregation
   of The United Methodist Church,
we renew our covenant
   faithfully to participate
   in the ministries of the church
   by our prayers, our presence,
   our gifts, and our service,
that in everything God may be glorified
   through Jesus Christ.**

BAPTISM WITH LAYING ON OF HANDS

As each candidate is baptized, the pastor says:

Name, I baptize you in the name of the Father, and of the Son, and of the Holy Spirit.

The people respond:

Amen.

Immediately after the administration of the water, the pastor, and others if desired, place hands on the head of each candidate, as the pastor says to each:

The Holy Spirit work within you,
that being born through water and the Spirit,
you may be a faithful disciple of Jesus Christ.

The people respond:

Amen.

When all candidates have been baptized, the pastor invites the congregation to welcome them:

Now it is our joy to welcome our new *sisters and brothers* in Christ.

Through baptism
you are incorporated by the Holy Spirit
into God's new creation
and made to share in Christ's royal priesthood.
We are all one in Christ Jesus.
With joy and thanksgiving we welcome you
as *members* of the family of Christ.

CONFIRMATION OR REAFFIRMATION OF FAITH

Here water may be used symbolically in ways that cannot be interpreted as baptism, as the pastor says:

Remember your baptism and be thankful.

Amen.

The pastor addresses those baptized, confirmed, or received:

The God of all grace,
who has called us to eternal glory in Christ,
establish you and strengthen you
by the power of the Holy Spirit,
that you may live in grace and peace.

One or more lay leaders may join with the pastor in acts of welcome and peace. . . .

1 Consecration of chrism 2 Rites preparatory to baptism 3 Baptismal rites 4 Rites preparatory to confirmation or post-baptismal rites 5 Imposition of hands and/or prayer for the Holy Spirit 6 Anointing with chrism or oil 7 Concluding rites

K. The Byzantine Rite of the Catholic Church
Baptism[446]

(Mass of Chrism precedes this celebration.)

1

RECEPTION INTO THE CATECHUMENATE....

EXORCISM....

PRAYER (WITH RENUNCIATION AND PROFESSION)....

2

BLESSING OF BAPTISMAL WATER....

BLESSING OF THE OIL OF CATECHUMENS....

THE ANOINTING....

3

THE BAPTISM....

THE CONFIRMATION

Priest: Let us pray to the Lord.
People: Lord, have mercy.

5

Priest: . . . O Master and Most Merciful King of all, grant him (her) also the Seal of the Gift of Your Holy, Almighty, and Adorable Spirit and the partaking of the most Holy Body and Precious Blood of Christ, Your Anointed One. Keep him (her) in Your sanctification, and strengthen him (her) in the Catholic Faith. Deliver him (her) from the Evil One and from all his cunning, and through a salutary fear of You preserve his (her) soul in purity and in righteousness, so that he (she) may please You in his (her) every word and deed, and thus may become a son (daughter) and heir to Your Heavenly Kingdom. . . .

J. The United Methodist Church
The Baptismal Covenant III
(Texts from the Former Methodist
and Former Evangelical United
Brethren Churches)[445]

INTRODUCTION TO THE SERVICE

A hymn may be sung.

The pastor makes the following statement to the congregation:

The church is of God,
and will be preserved to the end of time,
for the conduct of worship
and the due administration of God's Word and Sacraments,
the maintenance of Christian fellowship and discipline,
the edification of believers,
and the conversion of the world.
All, of every age and station,
stand in need of the means of grace which it alone supplies.

2

PRAYER FOR THOSE TO BE BAPTIZED....

RENUNCIATION OF SIN AND PROFESSION OF FAITH....

3

BAPTISM....

LAYING ON OF HANDS, CONFIRMATION, OR REAFFIRMATION
OF FAITH

As the pastor, or others if desired, place hands on the head of each person who has been baptized, or is being confirmed, or is reaffirming faith, the pastor says to each:

5

Name, the Lord defend you with his heavenly grace
and by his Spirit confirm you
in the faith and fellowship
of all true disciples of Jesus Christ.

The people respond:

Amen.

The priest dips his thumb into the Holy Chrism and resting his hand on the head of the one to be confirmed, he traces with his thumb the Sign of the Cross upon the forehead, then he proceeds to anoint the EYES, the NOSTRILS, the MOUTH, the EARS, the BREAST, the HANDS, and the FEET, saying at the same time but once:

THE SEAL OF THE GIFT ✚ OF THE HOLY SPIRIT.

Priest and people: Amen. . . .

Litany

Dismissal

1 Consecration of chrism 2 Rites preparatory to baptism 3 Baptismal rites 4 Rites preparatory to confirmation or post-baptismal rites 5 Imposition of hands and/or prayer for the Holy Spirit 6 Anointing with chrism or oil 7 Concluding rites

---

RECEPTION INTO THE UNITED METHODIST CHURCH. . . .

RECEPTION INTO THE LOCAL CONGREGATION. . . .

COMMENDATION AND WELCOME

Here a lay member, selected by the Administrative Board or Council, may join with the pastor in offering the hand of fellowship to all those received.

Then the pastor may have those received face the congregation and, causing the people to stand, address them, saying:

Brothers and sisters,
I commend to your love and care
    these persons whom we this day receive
    into the membership of this congregation.
Do all in your power
    to increase *their* faith,
confirm *their* hope,
    and perfect *them* in love.

The congregation responds:

We rejoice to recognize you
    as *members* of Christ's holy church,
and bid you welcome to this congregation
    of The United Methodist Church.
With you we renew our vows to uphold it
    by our prayers, our presence,
    our gifts, and our service.
With God's help we will so order our lives
    after the example of Christ
that, surrounded by steadfast love,
you may be established in the faith,
and confirmed and strengthened in the way
    that leads to life eternal.

The pastor may give a blessing.

Appendix II

Documentation

These twentieth century documents concern the age of confirmation and its sequence with first eucharist.

1. *Quam singulari*: Decree of the Sacred Congregation of the Discipline of the Sacraments on First Communion, August 8, 1910.

How singular was the love with which Christ attended the children on earth! The pages of the Gospel witness this clearly. . . .

Remembering these things, the Catholic Church, even from its beginnings, took care to draw children to Christ through eucharistic communion, which it used to administer even to infants. . . .

But over time not a few errors and woeful abuses have been introduced in establishing this age of reason or of discretion. . . . And therefore, for the sake of various customs of places and of peoples' opinions, in one place the age of ten or twelve years has been established for the first reception of eucharist, but in another the age of fourteen or even more, since children and young adolescents have been prohibited from eucharistic communion for a time, as the age has been prescribed. . . .

Since the ancients distributed the remains of the sacred species even to nursing children, there does not seem to be any just reason why an extraordinary preparation should now be demanded from children who abide in the most happy state of purity and innocence and greatly need that mystical food, because of so many temptations and dangers of this age. . . .

Therefore, as the age of discretion for confession is set at the time in which right from wrong may be distinguished, or at which one has arrived at a certain use of reason, so for communion it has been established to be at the time in which eucharistic bread can be discerned from ordinary bread—which, again, is the same age in which a child has attained the use of reason. . . .

Therefore a perfect knowledge of matters of faith is not required, since simply some rudiments are enough—that is, "some knowledge." Nor is a full use of reason required, since a certain beginning use of reason suffices—that is, "some use of reason." . . .

His Holiness Pope Pius X approved all these matters ratified by the cardinals of this holy congregation in an audience on the seventh day of the current month, and ordered the present decree to be published and promulgated. . . .[447]

2. *Age for Confirmation*: Sacred Congregation on Sacraments, June 30, 1932.

Many petitions have been sent to the Pontifical Commission for the Authentic Interpretation of the Code of Canon Law respecting the question of the age for confirmation as stated in c. 788, and the question whether the canon referred to is only a directive regulation or rather in fact mandatory.

Wherefore, the Eminent Fathers of this Pontifical Commission in plenary session on 7 June, 1931, considered the question: "Whether c. 788 is to be understood in the sense that the sacrament of confirmation cannot be conferred in the Latin Church before the age of about seven years, except in the cases mentioned in that canon." To which question they responded: "In the affirmative."[448]

Since, however, in Spain and other places, especially in South America, the custom has flourished of administering the sacrament of confirmation to children before the age of reason, and even immediately after baptism, a further question was provoked by this response, requesting the S. C. Sacr. to state whether such a custom could still be followed.

Therefore, in plenary session the Eminent Fathers of this Sacred Congregation on 27 Feb. 1932, after mature deliberation, considered this proposition:

Question. Whether the custom, very old in Spain and obtaining in other places, of administering the sacrament of confirmation to infants before the use of reason, can be followed.

Reply. The illustrious Fathers responded: In the affirmative, according to the mind of the Church; *et ad mentem*: the mind of the Church is that unless grave and just causes interfere, the administration of the sacrament of confirmation should be deferred until about the age of seven. According to c. 788, where a contrary custom prevails the faithful should be diligently taught the law of the Latin Church respecting the administration of the sacrament of confirmation after proper catechetical instruction, which, as experience teaches, helps to refine the minds of youth, and strengthens them in Catholic doctrine.

In the audience of 2 March, 1932, the undersigned Secretary of the Sacred Congregation received from His Holiness, Pius XI, the ratification and confirmation of this response.

Lest, however, from this decision any error should creep in or there should be any misunderstanding concerning the intention of the sacred canons and the precept about the age of those admitted for first Holy Communion, the same Sacred Congregation declared it was truly opportune and even more conformable to the nature and effects of the sacrament of confirmation, that children should not approach the sacred table for the first time unless after the reception of the sacrament of confirmation, which is, as it were, the complement of baptism and in which is given the fullness of the Holy Spirit (St. Thomas, III, q. 72, art. 2). They did not intend, however to keep from the sacred table those who heretofore have been admitted when they had reached the age of discretion, even though they had no opportunity of receiving the sacrament of confirmation previously.[449]

3. *Instruction for a Simple Priest Administering the Sacrament of Confirmation by Delegation from the Holy See*, Sacred Congregation on Sacraments, May 20, 1934.[450]

(*Part 3 concerns the age of confirmation. The congregation repeats the matter from June 30, 1932, then adds the following:*)

If therefore there is question of a child so seriously ill that he or she may be said to be in danger of death, not only is it not forbidden to administer Confirmation to him or her before the age of seven, but it is advisable to do so, so that upon leaving this life he or she may, according to the doctrine of Saint Thomas,[451] have greater glory in heaven. According to the approved opinion of several theologians,[452] in addition to the custom already mentioned, there may also be other legitimate reasons for anticipating the seventh year in the administration of this Sacrament, especially when it is foreseen that the Bishop or the priest who has faculty of administering it will be absent for a long time, or when there is some other necessity or just and serious reason.[453]

4. *Decree on Administering Confirmation to Those Who Have Been Established in Danger of Death from Grave Sickness,* Sacred Congregation on the Discipline of Sacraments, September 14, 1946.[454]
(This instruction includes the observation that many die before receiving confirmation, as was the case of many combatants in World War II. Then it praises the Eastern Churches' custom of celebrating the sacraments of initiation as one:)

Indeed this misfortune (that many die before receiving confirmation) is avoided in the Oriental Church, where there is a custom of confirming infants, immediately after the reception of baptism. Indeed the same discipline was in use in the first centuries of the church, even among Latins, and it is still preserved from a legitimate custom belonging to certain nations: however, the common law of the Latin Church, received in the cited canon 788, establishes that the administration of this sacrament be deferred to about the seventh year of age, at which time, after a uniform instruction of catechesis has been given, children share the richer effects of the sacrament.[455]

5. *Responses to Proposed Questions,* Pontifical Commission for Authentically Interpreting the Canons of the Code, March 26, 1952.[456]

III. Concerning the Age of Confirmands

Question: Whether, attentive to canon 788, the order of the bishop of a place may be sustained, which forbids that the sacrament of confirmation be administered to children who have not yet reached the age of ten years.

Answer: No.[457]

Notes

(1) I explain this term in chapter one.

(2) The official ritual book, the *Rite of Christian Initiation of Adults* (*RCIA*), was published for the United States in 1988. It is available from several publishers, including the United States Catholic Conference (Washington, D.C.), Liturgical Training Publications (Chicago), the Liturgical Press (Collegeville), and Catholic Book Publishing (New York).

(3) *RCIA* 215.

(4) *RCIA* 362–366.

(5) Gratian privately collected the laws of the church in the twelfth century. His efforts inspired further codifications throughout the middle ages. But not until 1917 did the Roman Catholic Church publish its own official code of law.

(6) Washington, D.C.: Canon Law Society of America.

(7) Canon 842/2.

(8) Appendix III in *RCIA*.

(9) Statute 14.

(10) See, for example, canon 891. Also, see canon 889/2: to be licitly confirmed the person should have "the use of reason." The *Rite of Confirmation* (*RC*) 12 uses the same expression. Canon 852/1: "What is prescribed in the canons on the baptism of an adult is applicable to all who are no longer infants but have attained the use of reason." Also, canon 913/1: to receive communion children should "have sufficient knowledge and careful preparation so as to understand the mystery of Christ according to their capacity and can receive the Body of the Lord with faith and devotion."

Canon 852/2 admits this exception for the developmentally

disabled: "One who is not of sound mind is equated with an infant so far as baptism is concerned."

(11) Canon 866.

(12) *RCIA*, Introduction, 2.

(13) *RCIA* 234.

(14) *RCIA* 233.

(15) Isaiah 11, 1–3.

(16) However, on February 17, 1973 The Sacred Congregation for the Evangelization of Nations or for the Propagation of the Faith gave permission to the Pro-Nuncio of Equatorial Guinea for the apostolic administrators of Bata and Santa Isabel to consecrate chrism that year, even though they were priests, not bishops. See *Canon Law Digest* (Chicago) 8:472–3.

(17) *Rite of Blessing of Oils and Consecrating the Chrism* 25, prayer A, found in Appendix II of the *Sacramentary*, or vol. 2 of *The Rites of the Catholic Church* (New York: Pueblo Publishing Co., 1980).

(18) Ibid., Consecratory Prayer B.

(19) See the second letter of St. Germanus of Paris in E. C. Whitaker, *Documents of the Baptismal Liturgy* (Slough: SPCK, 1970), p. 165.

(20) "The matter proper for the sacraments is olive oil or, according to circumstances, other plant oil. Chrism is made of oil and perfumes or other sweet smelling matter." *Rite of Blessing of Oils and Consecrating the Chrism*, 3–4.

(21) *RCIA* 235.

(22) *RCIA*, Introduction 2.

(23) *RCIA* 233.

(24) *RCIA*, Introduction 2.

(25) *RCIA* 215.

(26) Canon 852/1.

(27) *RCIA* 305.

(28) Statute 18.

(29) Cf. the *locus classicus, RCIA* 215.

(30) Canon 883/2.

(31) Canon 885/2.

(32) *Rite of Baptism for Children* 8/3, *The Rites*, vol. 1, 1976, p. 190.

(33) Canon 867/1.

(34) Some still fear that the child who dies before baptism will go to "limbo" because of original sin. Few theologians support the idea. It will be shown later that the Catholic funeral rites provide a ritual for the child who dies before baptism.

(35) Statute 19.

(36) See canon 866.

(37) *RCIA* 42.

(38) *RCIA* 75.

(39) *RCIA* 120.

(40) *RCIA* 138–139.

(41) *RCIA* 244.

(42) *RCIA* 252.

(43) *RCIA* 253.

(44) *RCIA* 23.

(45) *RC* 12.

(46) See *Lumen gentium* 26.

(47) Canon 882.

(48) See chapter 2.

(49) *The Code of Canon Law: A Text and Commentary*, ed. James A. Coriden, Thomas J. Green, and Donald E. Heintschel (New York: Paulist Press, 1985), p. 634. Hereafter, *Commentary*.

(50) Statute 11.

(51) Canon 883/2.

(52) *RCIA* 232.

(53) Canon 885/2.

(54) Statute 13.

(55) *RCIA* 231.

(56) *RCIA* 234.

(57) *RCIA* 235.

(58) Ibid.

(59) Ibid.

(60) Ibid.

(61) See, for example, the Rite of Acceptance into the Order of Catechumens, especially *RCIA* 50, and the optional rite of Giving of a New Name, *RCIA* 73.

(62) In the Rite of Election or Enrollment of Names, see *RCIA* 132.

(63) *RCIA* 226.

(64) Ibid.

(65) *RCIA* 240.
(66) *RCIA* 215.
(67) Canon 852/1.
(68) *RCIA* 12 and 207.
(69) Canon 863.
(70) Canon 1083/1.
(71) *RCIA* 24.
(72) *RCIA* 249.
(73) *RCIA* 215 and canon 866.
(74) *RCIA* 234. This is true of the English edition. The Latin original does not entitle this section at all, and the rubrics call for an imposition of hands.
(75) I treat this in more detail in chapter 5.
(76) See "Sacraments in the Eastern Churches" by Michael J. Fahey, S.J. in *The New Dictionary of Sacramental Worship*, ed. Peter E. Fink, S.J. (Collegeville: The Liturgical Press, 1990), pp. 1123–1124.
(77) *Orientalium Ecclesiarum*, 21 November 1964, 13, *Vatican Council II: The Conciliar and Post Conciliar Documents*, ed. Austin Flannery, O.P. (Collegeville: The Liturgical Press, 1975), pp. 445–446.
(78) Ibid., 14.
(79) David M. Petras, *Confirmation in the American Catholic Church: A Byzantine Perspective* (Washington: NCDD, 1980), pp. 25–27.
(80) Louis Ligier, *La Confirmation: Sens et conjoncture oecuménique hier et aujourd'hui* (Paris: Beauchesne, 1973), Théologie Historique 23, pp. 51–94.
(81) See Petras, p. 27. His note 119 reads, "Some translations are: Isabel Hapgood, *Service Book*, New York, 1965, 271–285; Fr. John von Holzhausen and Fr. Michael Gelsinger, *An Orthodox Prayer Book*, Brookline, Mass., 1977, 55–73; (both these translations are by the Orthodox Church, but give essentially the same rite as the Catholic). Catholic translations include: Joseph Sharry, "The Rite of Holy Baptism and Holy Chrismation" (private edition), Chicago, 1973, without pagination; *The Order of Baptism and Confirmation*, Byzantine Seminary Press, Pittsburgh, Pa., 1955."

(82) *The Order of Baptism and Confirmation According to The Byzantine Rite of the Catholic Church* (Pittsburgh: Byzantine Seminary Press, 1955), pp. 22–23.

(83) Ibid., p. 23.

(84) Canon 710, quoted below.

(85) Lucien Malouf, *Byzantine Melkite Thinking* (Beirut: Technogravure et Presse Libanaises, 1972), pp. 45–46.

(86) Trans. Archbishop Joseph Tawil, "The Theology of the Liturgy: The Three Sacraments of Christian Initiation" (West Newton: 1976). Again, various translations are available, including another from the Byzantine Ruthenian Province. The Greek original together with a Latin translation may be found in the works of R. P. Jacobi Goar, *Euchologion sive Rituale Graecorum complectens ritus et ordines Divinae Liturgiae, officiorum, sacramentorum, consecrationum, benedictionum, funerum, oratiunum, &c. cuilibet personae, statui, vel tempori congruos, juxta usum orientalis ecclesiae, cum selectis Bibliothecae Regiae, Barberinae, Cryptae-Ferratae, Sancti Marci Florentini, Tillianae, Allatianae, Coresianae, & aliis probatis MM. SS. & editis Exemplaribus collatum* (Venice: Typographia Bartholomae Javarina, 1730), p. 502.

(87) Ibid.

(88) Ibid.

(89) Ibid. Archbishop Tawil cites the following scriptural texts as fonts for this prayer: Jeremiah 9, 23; James 1, 17; Hebrews 3, 6; Psalms 44, 7; Titus 3, 5; Malachi 2, 16; 1 Corinthians 15, 53–54; Ephesians 2, 19; Psalms 105, 16; Titus 2, 14; Exodus 19, 5; Ephesians 3, 17; and Psalms 32, 14.

(90) Acts 8, 14–17 and 19, 1–6.

(91) E.g., Romans 8, 15; 1 Cor 2, 12; Gal 3, 2; Gal 4, 6; and 1 John 2, 27.

(92) E.g., 2 Cor 1, 21–22; Eph 1, 13–14; Eph 4, 30; and Heb 6, 1–2.

(93) Acts 10, 44–48.

(94) Frequently the ancient texts record the imposition of "a hand," instead of "hands." Apparently bishops of the early church often imposed a single hand according to the rituals.

(95) Aidan Kavanagh has argued that this ritual was actually a

dismissal rite presided over by the bishop. See *Confirmation: Origins and Reform* (New York: Pueblo, 1988), p. 70. I have responded to the book in "The Origins of Confirmation: An Analysis of Aidan Kavanagh's Hypothesis," *Worship* 65/4 (July 1991):320–336.

(96) About the year 390 Ambrose of Milan in *De mysteriis* (7, 42) tells his neophytes to recall that in their anointing, "Christ the Lord confirmed you and gave the spirit as a pledge in your hearts, as you have learned in the apostolic reading (2 Cor 1, 21–22)." But the verb had not yet become a title for the rite. For context, see Paul Turner, *Sources of Confirmation from the Fathers through the Reformers* (Collegeville: The Liturgical Press, 1993), #7.

(97) In Syria the anointing with chrism frequently preceded baptism. See Whitaker, pp. 21–59.

(98) See Turner, *Sources*, #94.

(99) Ibid., #83.

(100) Ligier, pp. 101–103.

(101) Ibid., p. 105.

(102) See Gabriele Winkler's summary in "Confirmation or Chrismation? A Study in Comparative Liturgy," *Worship* 58/1 (January, 1984):2–17.

(103) Winkler argues that the homily should be dated later than the fifth century Faustus. A parallel occurs in the collection of works by the seventh century Eusebius, so the original could be dated somewhere in between. See Turner, *Sources*, #56.

(104) William Bausch calls him "non-existent" in *A New Look at the Sacraments* (Mystic: Twenty-Third Publications, 1986), p. 99; so does Joseph Martos in *Doors to the Sacred*, expanded edition (Tarrytown: Triumph Books, 1991), p. 188. There really was a Pope Melchiades, an African and a saint, who served from 311 to 314 A.D., a short but critical period during which the Emperor Constantine issued the Edict of Milan which set Christianity free in the empire. Melchiades, of course, died centuries before the work attributed to him was written.

(105) Cyril of Jerusalem, *Third Mystagogical Catechesis* 3,3. Translations include *The Awe-Inspiring Rites of Initiation: Baptismal Homilies of the Fourth Century*, trans. Edward Yarnold, S.J. (Slough: St. Paul Publications, 1971).

(106) Petras, p. 7.

(107) See Casimir Kucharek's *The Sacramental Mysteries: A Byzantine Approach* (Allendale: Alleluia Press, 1976), pp. 131–132.

(108) The Greek term for the seal is *sphragis.*

(109) The *Codex canonum ecclesiarum Orientalium* is published in the *Acta Apostolicae Sedis* (AAS) 82/11 (18 October 1990). Canon 697 is cited here. See also *Code of Canons of the Eastern Churches* (Washington, D.C.: Canon Law Society of America, 1992).

(110) Ibid., canon 710.

(111) Petras, pp. 12–15.

In Clemente Pujol's "Commentary" on the Code of Oriental Law, he points out the pastoral importance of catechesis for this sacrament: "As to the sacrament of confirmation or chrismation, since it is generally administered by the Orientals at the same time as baptism, it presents a danger that the faithful might lightly ignore this sacrament, nor be conscious of the effects which are produced in the baptized through it. Therefore it is fitting that the pastor or minister of baptism explain to the faithful the importance of this sacrament in the life of the baptized." *Notitiae* 292 (November 1990):681.

(112) Petras, p. 1.

(113) Ibid., p. 28.

(114) Alkiviadis C. Calivas, "The Sacramental Life in the Orthodox Church," from *A Companion to the Greek Orthodox Church,* ed. Fotios K. Litsas (New York: Greek Orthodox Archdiocese of North and South America, 1990), p. 39.

(115) A synopsis of texts chosen for this chapter appears in Appendix II.

(116) I have treated this material in more detail in *The Meaning and Practice of Confirmation: Perspectives from a Sixteenth Century Controversy* (Bern: Peter Lang, 1987), pp. 7–35.

(117) *De captivitate Babylonica ecclesiae praeludium,* found in *D. Martin Luthers Werke. Kritische Gesammtausgabe* (Weimar: Hermann Böhlau, 1883) 6:549.

(118) "Predigt am Sonntag Lätare Nachmittags (15. März 1523)," WA 11:66. This text can be found in Turner, *Sources,* #26, together with other similar passages by Luther.

(119) A helpful text is Frak W. Klos, *Confirmation and First Communion: A Study Book* (Minneapolis: Augsburg Publishing House, 1968).

(120) *Lutheran Book of Worship* (Minneapolis: Augsburg Publishing House, 1982), p. 198, #3.

(121) Ibid., p. 201, #14.

(122) Ibid.

(123) Ibid.

(124) Ibid., p. 124, #13.

(125) Ibid., #14.

(126) Philip H. Pfatteicher and Carlos R. Messerli, *Manual on the Liturgy: Lutheran Book of Worship* (Minneapolis: Augsburg Publishing House, 1979), p. 340.

(127) Quoted in Pfatteicher and Messerli, p. 340.

(128) Ibid., pp. 340–341.

(129) Ibid., p. 341.

(130) *Lutheran Worship* (St. Louis: Concordia Publishing House).

(131) Ibid., pp. 206–207, #2.

(132) Ibid., p. 207, #3.

(133) Ibid., #4.

(134) Ibid., p. 203, #14.

(135) Supplemental Liturgical Resource 2, prepared by The Office of Worship for the Presbyterian Church (U.S.A.) and the Cumberland Presbyterian Church (Philadelphia: The Westminster Press, 1985).

(136) Ibid., p. 69.

(137) A "session" is a governing committee of a particular Presbyterian congregation.

(138) Part II, The Book of Order (Louisville: The Office of the General Assembly, 1991), W–4.2003.

(139) Ibid., p. 76.

(140) Ibid.

(141) Ibid., pp. 76–77.

(142) Ibid., p. 77.

(143) Ibid.

(144) Ibid., p. 31.

(145) Ibid.

(146) From "An Outline of the Faith," the Catechism in *The Book of Common Prayer and Administration of the Sacraments and Other Rites and Ceremonies of the Church* (New York: The Church Hymnal Corporation, 1979), p. 860.

(147) See Gerard Austin, *The Rite of Confirmation: Anointing with the Spirit*, pp. 67–78 *passim*.

(148) Title I, canon 17, sec. 1c, from *Constitution & Canons for the Government of the Protestant Episcopal Church in the United States of America, Otherwise Known as the Episcopal Church, adopted in General Conventions 1789–1991, Together with the Rules of Order*, rev. 1991 (no publication data).

(149) *The Book of Common Prayer*, p. 412.

(150) Ibid., pp. 420–421.

(151) Ibid., p. 417.

(152) Ibid., p. 418.

(153) *The Book of Common Prayer* places masculine pronouns in italics to represent the presider's responsibility to use the appropriate gender. Plural pronouns in italics may be made singular in either gender if the ritual is performed for one person instead of many.

(154) *The Book of Common Prayer*, p. 418.

(155) Ibid., p. 307.

(156) Ibid., p. 308.

(157) Ibid.

(158) *Constitution & Canons*, title I, canon 17, sec. 1d.

(159) Hoyt L. Hickman, *United Methodist Worship* (Nashville: Abingdon Press, 1991), pp. 99–100.

(160) *The Book of Discipline of the United Methodist Church, 1988* (Nashville: The United Methodist Publishing House, 1988), p. 114, #106.

(161) Ibid., pp. 126–127, #216.

(162) *The United Methodist Hymnal: Book of United Methodist Worship* (Nashville: The United Methodist Publishing House, 1990), p. 32.

(163) Ibid., p. 37, #12.

(164) Ibid., #12.

(165) Ibid., p. 39, #16.

(166) Ibid., p. 37.

(167) Ibid., p. 47.

(168) See *RCIA* 400, and the Commission for Interpretation of Decrees of Vatican II, Dec. 21, 1979, I, 2: AAS 72 (1980), 105.

The code of canon law reserves the confirmation of the second group of candidates to the bishop. The *Commentary* on canon 883 observes, "This limitation, unaffected by the canon, creates an anomalous situation at the Easter Vigil, if such persons are then admitted to full practice. Bishops have therefore sought indults from the Apostolic See to permit presbyteral confirmation for this occasion or have invoked other principles of the canon law. The norm, however, is as stated above," p. 636.

(169) The *Rite of Reception of Baptized Christians into Full Communion with the Catholic Church* was published independent of the *RCIA* in 1976. This rite is now contained within the 1988 publication of the *RCIA*, #473–504.

(170) *RCIA* 491 and 585.

(171) *RCIA* 492 and 586.

(172) *RCIA* 252–330.

(173) *RCIA* 400–472.

(174) Canon 883/2.

(175) Canon 885/2. The *Commentary* on this canon observes, "Thus the presbyter who baptizes a person who is no longer an infant or receives a baptized person of such an age into full communion should not fail to confirm him or her on that occasion," p. 637.

RCIA 308 supports the same conclusion: "When the bishop himself will not be the celebrant, he should grant the faculty to confirm (baptized) children to the priest who will be the celebrant."

However, the *Rite of Confirmation* (7b) makes it ambiguous where it has the opportunity to be clear: "In addition to the bishop, the law gives the faculty to confirm to . . . priests who, in virtue of an office which they lawfully hold, baptize an adult or a child old enough for catechesis or receive a validly baptized adult into full communion with the Church." The confirmation of a validly baptized child is not mentioned. Perhaps this is why *RCIA* 308 suggests the bishop should grant the priest the faculty in those cases.

(176) *Lumen gentium* 14.

(177) See Petras, p. 26.

(178) I differentiate between "orthodox" and "Orthodox" throughout this chapter and the book. "Orthodox," as opposed to "Catholic," describes the Eastern Rites not in union with Rome since 1054; "orthodox," opposed to heresy and schism, refers to

the unified early Christian church in the first few centuries after Christ.

(179) "Heresy is the obstinate post-baptismal denial of some truth which must be believed with divine and Catholic faith, or it is likewise an obstinate doubt concerning the same; apostasy is the total repudiation of the Christian faith; schism is the refusal of submission to the Roman Pontiff or of communion with the members of the Church subject to him." Canon 751.

"With due regard for can. 194/1, n. 2, an apostate from the faith, a heretic or a schismatic incurs automatic excommunication. . . ." Canon 1364/1.

(180) Ligier, pp. 157–161.

(181) In extreme cases heretics were baptized if the church did not accept their baptism.

(182) Ligier, p. 161.

(183) A similar distinction of themes could be made for confirmation within baptismal initiation and delayed confirmation. The first stresses the gift of the Spirit in initiation; the second, delayed by some years, stresses strengthening with the Spirit for those who have been enjoying the merits of the Christian life.

(184) In fairness, the Anglican communion is divided on this point. Some churches hold the same seven sacraments as Roman and Eastern Catholics, but others honor only baptism and eucharist with the title.

(185) Members of Eastern Rites in union with Rome, of course, already share communion with the Roman Rite. If they wish to join the Roman Rite they do so through a transfer of membership, not through a profession of faith and certainly not through confirmation.

(186) See "Decree on Ecumenism" (*Unitatis redintegratio*, 21 November 1964), n. 15, and Section V of "On Admitting Other Christians to Eucharistic Communion in the Catholic Church" (*In quibus rerum circumstantiis*, 1 June 1972), AAS 64: 518–525, and collections of the documents of Vatican II.

(187) See the code of Oriental law, canon 897.

(188) Ibid., canon 36.

(189) Ibid., canon 32.

(190) Ibid., canon 31. Such action provokes a penalty in canon 1465.

(191) Ibid., canon 29.

(192) Ibid., canon 30.

(193) As a general rule. There are pastoral exceptions.

(194) Timothy Ware, *The Orthodox Church* (Harmondsworth: Penguin Books, 1973), pp. 285–286. And Clement C. Englert, *Catholics and Orthodox: Can They Unite?* (New York: Paulist Press, 1961), p. 49. See also Fahey, p. 1127.

(195) In the Catholic parallel, a priest confirms returning apostates if they have not previously been confirmed. See *Commentary*, p. 636, n. 254. There is no second celebration of confirmation.

(196) Calivas, p. 39.

(197) It used to be more serious. "A synod at Constantinople in 1755 . . . decreed that Latin and Armenian baptisms were invalid and converts must be rebaptized according to the Byzantine rite of triple immersion before they could be admitted to the Church. Thus the strictest regulations regarding the admission of heretics to the Church were now applied to Roman Catholics and Monophysite Armenians." John Meyendorff, *The Orthodox Church: Its Past and Its Role in the World Today*, trans. John Chapin (New York: Pantheon Books, 1962), pp. 97–98.

(198) It's not surprising, then, that many involved in the confirmation of adolescents erroneously regard the ceremony as "joining the Catholic Church." That is one interpretation of the sacrament, if the person being confirmed was baptized in another church.

(199) A Protestant woman asked me recently if she could receive communion in our parish without being confirmed. "That's what you do with Catholic children," she reasoned.

(200) Admittedly, this is the Catholic perspective.

(201) The irrepeatable nature of chrismation/confirmation is affirmed in the code of Oriental law, canon 672/1, and in the Roman code, canon 889/1.

(202) *Sacrosanctum concilium* 71.

(203) Prot. n. 800/71, published in *RC*. The Decree is signed by Arturo Cardinal Tabera, prefect, and Annibale Bugnini, secretary.

(204) Bernard Botte says the text was actually prepared by Père Dhanis, a Belgian Jesuit at the Gregorian University in Rome, and

Père Gy. *From Silence to Participation*, trans. John Sullivan, O.C.D. (Washington, D.C.: The Pastoral Press, 1988), p. 161.

(205) *RC* 13.

(206) *Sacrosanctum concilium* 71.

(207) Canon 884/2.

(208) Botte, p. 158.

(209) *Sacrosanctum concilium* 71.

(210) Apostolic Constitution on the Sacrament of Confirmation.

(211) *RC* 1.

(212) *RC* 7–8.

(213) *RC* 11.

(214) *RC* 12.

(215) Ibid.

(216) Apostolic Constitution.

(217) This expression could argue in favor of the traditional sequence of the sacraments of initiation: baptism-confirmation-eucharist. The Constitution implies that the arrangement of the sacraments, even when they are not celebrated together, expresses the unity of initiation. The Latin text follows: "Vinculum autem, quo Confirmatio cum reliquis eiusmodi Sacramentis sociatur, non solum ex eo apertius innotescit, quod *ritus arctiore nexu dispositi sunt*, sed apparet etiam e gestu et verbis, quibus Confirmatio ipsa confertur." (Emphasis mine.) *Ordo confirmationis* (Vatican City: Typis Polyglottis Vaticanis, 1973).

(218) *RC* 12.

(219) Ibid.

(220) Ibid.

(221) See, for example, the role of sponsor outlined at #5 and the sample general intercession for parents and sponsors at #30, which prays that those who led the confirmands in faith "may always encourage them to follow the way of Jesus Christ."

(222) *RC* 5. Also canon 893/2.

(223) *RC* 6. Canon 893/1 says, "To perform the role of sponsor, it is necessary that a person fulfill the conditions mentioned in can. 874."

Canon 874/1 gives the requirements for a baptismal sponsor. "To be admitted to the role of sponsor, a person must:

"1) be designated by the one to be baptized, by the parents or the one who takes their place or, in their absence, by the pastor or minister and is to have qualifications and intention of performing this role;

"2) have completed the sixteenth year, unless a different age has been established by the diocesan bishop or it seems to the pastor or minister that an exception is to be made for a just cause;

"3) be a Catholic who has been confirmed and has already received the sacrament of the Most Holy Eucharist and leads a life in harmony with the faith and the role to be undertaken;

"4) not be bound by any canonical penalty legitimately imposed or declared;

"5) not be the father or the mother of the one to be baptized."

A conflict seems to arise between this last provision and the statement from *RC* 5 that "Even the parents themselves may present their children for confirmation." The *Commentary* on canon 893 states that "the parents in such instances would not be sponsors in the strictest sense," p. 642, citing a report to the Pontifical Commission on the Code of Canon Law in *Relatio complectens synthesim animadversionum ab Em. mis. atque Exc. mis. Patribus Commissionis ad ultimum schema Codicis Iuris Canonici Exhibitarum, cum responsionibus a Secretaria et Consultoribus datis* (Vatican City: Typis Polyglottis Vaticanis, 1981), p. 209.

(224) *RC* 21.
(225) *RC* 26.
(226) *RC* 24.
(227) *RC* 22.
(228) *RC* 11.
(229) *RC* 13.
(230) *RC* 13.
(231) *RC* 31.
(232) *RC* 32.
(233) *RC* 27.
(234) See Kucharek's treatment of this point, pp. 180–181.
(235) See the Decree and *Lumen gentium* 11.
(236) Apostolic Constitution.
(237) Ibid.
(238) Quoting here from *De resurrectione mortuorum*, 8, 3.
(239) *RC* 35.

(240) *Lumen gentium* 11.

(241) *RC* 24.

(242) Joseph Campbell argues that the slap represents the dying and rising motif: One takes the blow in order to rise stronger again. See *The Hero with a Thousand Faces*, Bollingen Series XVII (Princeton: Princeton University Press, 1949), third printing 1973, p. 143.

(243) *RC* 2.

(244) *RC* 24.

(245) *RC* 27.

(246) *RC* 9.

(247) *RC* 22.

(248) *RC* 58.

(249) *RC* 59.

(250) *RC* 33.

(251) Decree.

(252) *RC* 2.

(253) *RC* 7.

(254) *RC* 9.

(255) *RC* 22.

(256) *RC* 23.

(257) *RC* 30.

(258) *RC* 33.

(259) *RC* 35.

(260) *RC* 59.

(261) Decree. See also the Apostolic Constitution, the suggested homily (22), the prayer for the imposition of hands (24), and the insert for Eucharistic Prayer I ("Father, accept this offering from those . . . confirmed by the coming of the Holy Spirit," 58).

(262) *RC* 22.

(263) See intercessions (#30) and blessing (#33).

(264) See the first opening prayer (#35) and the communion prayers (#59 and #60).

(265) See #9 and #25.

(266) See #9 and #27.

(267) *RC* 27.

(268) *RC* 23. The usual threefold questions (e.g. in the *Rite of Baptism for Children* 58) are thus expanded to four.

(269) *RC* 13.

(270) See Apostolic Constitution and *Lumen gentium* 11.

(271) *RC* 3.

(272) *RC* 27 and 32.

(273) *RC* 3.

(274) Ibid.

(275) *RC* 26.

(276) *RC* 30.

(277) *RC* 7.

(278) *RC* 4.

(279) *RC* 29.

(280) For example, alternative versions of the renunciation of sin and profession of faith, the sign of peace, and the celebrant's explanations of the liturgy. *RC* 16–18.

(281) *RC* 14.

(282) *RC* 15.

(283) *RC* 19.

(284) *RC* 30 and 60.

(285) *RC* 58.

(286) *RC* 59.

(287) *RC* 22.

(288) In the rite, see #1.

(289) Hebrews 6, 2.

(290) *RC* 7.

(291) Even when other priests assist the bishop, they may impose hands but the bishop alone recites the prayer (*RC* 9).

(292) *RC* 10.

(293) *RC* 28.

(294) *RC* 13.

(295) *RC* 22.

(296) *RC* 11.

(297) Ibid.

(298) Annibale Bugnini, *The Liturgical Reform, 1948–1975*, trans. Matthew J. O'Connell (Collegeville: The Liturgical Press, 1990), p. 614.

(299) Botte, p. 156.

(300) See, for example, Terri McKenzie and Michael J. Savelesky, "Confirmation with First Communion? It Works!" *Chicago Catechumenate* (May 1986):16–23.

(301) Bugnini, p. 621, n. 19.

(302) *RC* 5.

(303) *Sharing the Light of Faith: National Catechetical Directory for Catholics of the United States* (Washington: U.S. Catholic Conference, 1979), #119.

(304) *RC* 25.

(305) AAS 64 (1972):526. Cited in Austin, pp. 45 and 61.

(306) References to Acts 8 in relation to confirmation first appeared after it had already separated from baptism. See Kavanagh, *Confirmation: Origins and Reform*, pp. 56ff.

(307) Canon 1065/1.

(308) Canon 1033.

(309) Canon 645/1.

(310) Canon 874/3.

(311) Canon 893/1.

(312) See, for example, *RC*: the Decree from the Office of Divine Worship, Paul VI's Apostolic Constitution, and the Introduction #1.

(313) See, for example, Martos, "Some Weaknesses in the 'Restored Sequence' Argument," *Gifts* 1 (1991):6–7.

(314) See Martos' comments in "Confirmation at the Crossroads," *The Living Light* 28/3 (Spring 1992):232.

(315) AAS 2:577–583. See Appendix I for this and other texts.

(316) See Linda Gaupin, "Now Confirmation Needs Its Own *Quam singulari*," in *When Should We Confirm?* ed. James A. Wilde (Chicago: Liturgical Training Publications, 1989), pp. 85–93.

(317) *RC* 11.

(318) Bishops' Committee on the Liturgy, "Decisions of the National Conference of Catholic Bishops: Age for Confirmation," *Newsletter* 8/5 & 6 (May-June 1972):326–7.

(319) Canon 891.

(320) See *Commentary* on canon 891, p. 639.

(321) Canon 889/2.

(322) The NCCB learned in late 1991 that the Vatican's Congregation for Bishops could not approve their proposal. Cardinal Gantin wrote "that the Holy See has a difficulty in confirming this decision because only two age options are presented in the Code: either the approximate age of discretion . . . or another age decided upon by the Episcopal Conference" (Letter to Archbishop

Daniel E. Pilarczyk, Prot. N. 296/84, Vatican City, November 26, 1991).

(323) *Cuius regio eius confirmatio*, so to speak.

(324) Jerry Filteau, "Confirmation Age Left Up to Each Bishop," *Catholic News Service* (November 14, 1984).

(325) Thomas H. Groome's *Christian Religious Education: Sharing Our Story and Vision* (San Francisco: Harper and Row, 1980) offers a fuller treatment.

(326) Michael Warren has suggested that confirmations forced upon young people should be annulled like failed marriages. Quoted in Thomas A. Marsh, et al., *Confirming the Faith of Adolescents*, Arthur J. Kubick, ed. (New York: Paulist Press, 1991), p. 7.

(327) I have distilled this construction from many sources. The literature on adolescent confirmation is scattered through hundreds of articles in dozens of journals and innumerable books and catechetical texts. Others may formulate a different reconstruction of the basic principles. There is no single source one can turn to. For a more expanded summary of the position, see Arthur J. Kubick's "Introduction" to *Confirming the Faith of Adolescents*, p. 4.

(328) See Kieran Sawyer, "A Case for Adolescent Confirmation," in *Confirming the Faith of Adolescents*: "The sacraments of initiation must be received freely," p. 28.

(329) Sawyer writes, "Thus infant baptism focuses on the faith of the church and the gift dimension of the initiation reality, while confirmation focuses on the personal faith of the individual and the commitment dimensions of initiation," p. 41.

(330) Marsh says, "Membership of the church means essentially the mature member, the person capable of professing mature faith," "Christian Initiation: Practice and Theology," *Confirming the Faith of Adolescents*, p. 20.

(331) Most would renew their baptismal promises only if they were chosen to be godparents for an infant's baptism. The renewal of promises at the Easter Vigil came with the reforms of Vatican II, and its inclusion at all Masses Easter Sunday is an approved adaptation for the Catholic Church in the United States.

(332) See, for example, "Confirmation for Commitment to

Mission," by Eric Doyle, O.F.M., in *The Clergy Review* 67/5 (May, 1982):162–165.

(333) *Summa theologica* III, q. 72, art. 5.

(334) See Sawyer, pp. 36–41.

(335) Sawyer says, "The goal of Christian initiation is mature faith," p. 29.

(336) Referring to confirmed children who have not achieved a mature, fully-committed faith, Sawyer says, "Even though they have received the initiation sacraments, such children will not be fully initiated," p. 39.

(337) Sawyer disagrees with this point. "The culmination of the initiation process is the Eucharist. . . . (Each) reception of eucharist 'completes' initiation." She argues that no matter when confirmation happens, eucharist culminates initiation, pp. 34–35.

(338) In *Confirming the Faith of Adolescents* see Craig Cox, "Rethinking Confirmation: Possible Ways Forward," pp. 170ff, and Bernard Cooke, "An Afterword," p. 183. Cooke favors one confirmation followed by other rites of passage; Cox favors a "confirmation by stages" across many years of life's journey.

(339) See Winkler, and Frank Quinn's "Theology of Confirmation" in *The New Dictionary of Sacramental Worship*, p. 277, where he cites canon 3 of the Council of Riez (439) and canon 2 of the Council of Orange (441).

(340) See this argument in the two articles by Martos: "Crossroads":230 and "Weaknesses":5.

(341) See Martos, "Crossroads":238.

(342) See, for example, Rembert Weakland's introduction to Sawyer's book *Confirming Faith* (Notre Dame: Ave Maria Press, 1982).

(343) Both Jerome and Pope Innocent I introduced the argument that since the apostles imposed hands sometime after baptism, confirmation may stand as an independent ritual. Prior to this time references to Acts do not appear in the literature surrounding the post-baptismal anointing and/or imposition of hands. Both texts may be found in Turner, *Sources*, #101 and #95.

(344) See Turner, *The Meaning and Practice of Confirmation*, pp. 251–262.

(345) Marsh pushes this farther in his claim that Acts 2, 38 also

signifies a division in early Christian initiation practice. In "Confirmation in Scripture," his article in *The New Dictionary of Sacramental Worship*, he notes that Peter's admonition to repent and be baptized is followed by a promise, "you will receive the gift of the Holy Spirit." Marsh argues that this promise pertains to a future rite, distinct from baptism—namely, the imposition of hands. He seems alone in this interpretation.

(346) These hypotheses recall those of the counter-Reformation. Robert Bellarmine tried to prove that apostles not only imposed hands but also anointed the newly baptized with chrism. He says the reason Luke does not say so explicitly is that he was simply abridging the text. See Turner, *The Meaning and Practice of Confirmation*, pp. 252–253.

(347) See Marsh, "Christian Initiation: Practice and Theology," in *Confirming the Faith of Adolescents*, p. 18.

(348) Marsh, however, generalizes the experience of Acts: "St. Luke's description of this system in Acts has to be accepted as historically accurate." "Christian Initiation: Practice and Theology," p. 18.

(349) Kubick surveys some "RCIA-inspired preparation" materials in "Confirmation at St. Elizabeth's Parish: A Reflection," in *Confirming the Faith of Adolescents*, p. 79.

(350) *RCIA* 75.

(351) *RC* 24.

(352) *RC* 9.

(353) For example, Sawyer, "A Case for Adolescent Confirmation," p. 42. See comments on this interpretation in the first chapter.

(354) *RC* 12.

(355) Ibid.

(356) This is why Sawyer says that the desire to celebrate weekly eucharist is "THE" criterion for readiness for adolescent confirmation. See *Confirming Faith*, p. 9.

(357) *RCIA* 400–410.

(358) Sawyer, "A Case for Adolescent Confirmation," p. 42.

(359) Canon 777/2.

(360) E.g., canons 842/2, 874/1, and the very order of materials in Book IV, Part I, Titles I, II, and III (Baptism, Confirmation, and The Most Holy Eucharist). Vatican II's Decree on the

Church's Missionary Activity (*Ad gentes*) follows the adult sequence at #36.

(361) Like the expression in the Decree, this canon represents an isolated case of the alternate sequence.

(362) *Rite of Baptism for Children* 3.

(363) E.g., Sawyer, "Confirmation Dilemma: A Conflict of Principles," *Gifts* (Winter, 1990):3.

(364) *Sacrosanctum concilium* 14.

(365) A strange twist, given the whole thrust of *Quam singulari*.

(366) E.g., Sawyer, "Confirmation Dilemma":2.

(367) Theresa Viramontes-Gutierrez offers a very few resources in her article, "A Look at Confirmation Through 'Spanish' Eyes," *Confirming the Faith of Adolescents*, p. 106.

(368) Martos maintains the Orthodox become non-participants as frequently as Catholics do, "Weaknesses":7.

(369) Petras, p. 30.

(370) I am grateful to Kieran Sawyer for collecting these references.

(371) *Christ the Sacrament of the Encounter with God* (New York: Sheed and Ward, 1963), p. 161.

(372) Rahner and Herbert Vorgrimler, *Theological Dictionary*, 1965 ed., s.v. "Confirmation." However, note in the second edition (1981) the addition of this sentence at the end of the same article: "Liturgical interests would like to restore the ancient process of Christian initiation: baptism, confirmation, Eucharist."

(373) *Encyclopedia of Theology: the Concise* Sacramentum Mundi, ed. Karl Rahner, s.v. "Confirmation" (New York: The Seabury Press, 1975).

(374) *Holy Spirit of God* (London: G. Chapman, 1986), p. 95.

(375) *The Sacraments Today* (Maryknoll: Orbis, 1974), p. 41, n. 7.

(376) *I Believe in the Holy Spirit*, trans. David Smith, vol. 3 (London: G. Chapman, 1983), p. 224. However, Congar says this is one of two interpretations, the other that confirmation is a sacrament of initiation linked closer to baptism. He concludes, "In my opinion, both the first and the second views outlined above contain truths that should be respected. . . . Both truths should be given a place and the special attributes of each respected."

(377) *Sacraments and Sacramentality* (Mystic, Connecticut: Twenty-Third Publications, 1988), p. 146.

(378) Ibid., p. 147.

(379) Foreword to Sawyer's *Confirming Faith*, p. 5.

(380) *Confirming Faith*, p. 9.

(381) John Roberto's oft-cited paper, "Confirmation in the American Catholic Church" (Washington: NCDD, 1978), records the early establishment of these schools.

The two camps rarely see eye-to-eye. Off the printed page one frequently finds antagonism redolent of the Reformation, where those who believed confirmation was not a sacrament and those who believed it was vehemently denounced each other with colorful language. For example, in response to the Council of Trent's decree that bishops are the ordinary minister of confirmation, John Calvin railed, "And certainly the horned and mitred asses are worthy of such a privilege. For what should they do when they are no more fit for fulfilling the episcopal office than pigs are for singing?" See Turner, *Sources*, #133.

(382) McKenzie and Savelesky record their frustrations with confirming adolescents in "Confirmation with First Communion? It Works!" where they write that "helping adolescents relate to confirmation . . . seemed inappropriate and unfair."

See also McKenzie's "Restoring the Sequence of the Sacraments of Initiation" in *PACE* 21:119–122. She writes, "Is the sacrament of confirmation of so little value that the church could afford to have so many not celebrating it? . . . If confirmation is the sacrament of service . . . how could we explain the notable lack of participation in any aspect of church service which so often followed the celebration of the sacrament? If confirmation is the sacrament of commitment, why does it come to be more of a graduation ceremony—signaling the end of the young persons' religious education—and often their attendance at church?"

(383) Anthropologically, one might say that adult baptism is "inter-tribal" initiation and infant baptism is "intra-tribal" initiation.

(384) "Even though uncatechized adults have not yet heard the message of the mystery of Christ, their status differs from that of catechumens, since by baptism they have already become members of the Church and children of God. Hence their conver-

sion is based on the baptism they have already received, the effects of which they must develop." RCIA 400.

(385) Evangelii nuntiandi, 8 December 1975. Found, among other places, in Vatican Council II: More Postconciliar Documents, ed. Austin Flannery, O.P., vol. 2, p. 711.

(386) Ibid., #27, translation adapted.

(387) Ibid., #18, translation adapted.

(388) Ibid., #15, translation adapted.

(389) Statute 2.

(390) John Calvin warned against this in the sixteenth century. In his Antidote to the Council of Trent, he wrote ("On Confirmation," 1) that bishops "claim that baptism suffices for those soon about to die, but those who will be prevailing are armed with confirmation that they be able to sustain the struggles. So a half part of efficacy is lopped off from baptism, as if it were said for nothing that the old person is crucified in baptism, so that we may walk in newness of life (Rom 6:6)." See Turner, Sources, #79.

(391) Rite of Baptism for Children 3.

(392) "Pastoralis actio," 20 October 1980, #31, found among other places in Vatican Council II, vol. 2, pp. 103–117.

(393) Canon 868/2.

(394) Canon 889/2.

(395) See, for example, "Pastoral Statement of the United States Catholic Bishops on Handicapped People: A Statement Issued by the United States Catholic Conference, November 15, 1978," #24. This document may be found, among other places, in National Conference of Catholic Bishops and United States Catholic Conference, Pastoral Letters of the United States Catholic Bishops, Vol. 4: 1975–1983, ed. Hugh J. Nolan (Washington: USCC, 1984), p. 272.

(396) Canon 852/2.

(397) The requirements apply only "if the person has the use of reason," Canon 889/2. The RC 12 uses the same phrase.

(398) The bishops of Spain recently argued that confirmation should be perceived primarily as a gift of God, and secondarily as a "response of the believer who has the use of reason." They have set the national age for confirmation at the age of discretion, "so that (the children) may receive consciously and responsibly the gift of God and accept the obligations which the Christian life

brings with it." See p. 578 of "Conferentiae Episcoporum: Hispania: Nota de la Comision Episcopal para la Doctrina de la Fe sobre Algunos Aspectos Doctrinales del Sacramento de la confirmacion," *Notitiae* 303 (October 1991):576–582.

(399) For many teens confirmation runs neck and neck with penance as the least-loved sacrament in the Catholic Church.

(400) A baby born to a Christian household already shares membership in the church. The death of a child before baptism used to cause grave concern for Christian parents. The revised funeral liturgy now includes the burial rites for the child who dies before baptism. (See the *Order of Christian Funerals*, available from several publishers, #237 and #254c, for example.) The funeral liturgy treats this child as a member of the Christian family. No commitment needed.

(401) *RCIA* 252–330.

(402) *RCIA* 252.

(403) *RCIA* 252.

(404) *RCIA* 217.

(405) Even the Roman Missal's second preface for the Holy Eucharist (P 48) says the faithful come to the eucharist to "grow into the likeness of the risen Christ" (New York: Catholic Book Publishing Co., 1985), p. 469. Confirmation language again.

(406) *RCIA* 243.

(407) *Commentary*, p. 632.

(408) The opening paragraph of the Decree preceding the Rite of Confirmation and canon 777.

(409) These followed the decree *Quam singulari*. See AAS 24 (1932):271–272; 27 (1935):15; and 44 (1952):496. AAS 38 (1946):350 praises the custom in the Eastern Rites. See Appendix II of this book, and two articles in *Confirmed as Children, Affirmed as Teens*: Austin, "Eucharist and the Confirmation Debate," p. 21, and Richard P. Moudry, "A Parish Resource for Confirmation: What Does Vatican II Say?" p. 29.

(410) Canon 879.

(411) Canon 889/1.

(412) Canon 672/1.

(413) In *Celebrating Confirmation* (Winona: Saint Mary's Press, 1990), Thomas Zanzig concludes his summary of New Testament origins asserting, "the roots of the sacrament can be found in the

laying on of hands and in an anointing occasionally mentioned in the context of baptism and related specifically to the gift of the Spirit."

(414) 1 Kings 3, 16–28.

(415) *RC* 52–56.

(416) *RC* 52.

(417) *Pastoral Care of the Sick: Rites of Anointing and Viaticum,* #246.

(418) *RC* 52.

(419) Ibid.

(420) *Pastoral Care of the Sick* 175.

(421) *RC* 53.

(422) *RC* 54–55.

(423) *RC* 56.

(424) *RC* 52.

(425) *Pastoral Care of the Sick* 238.

(426) See canon 883/3.

(427) See *RCIA* 372 and 385, and *Pastoral Care of the Sick* 276.

(428) Canon 890.

(429) *RC* 11.

(430) *Order of Christian Funerals* 220.

(431) *RCIA* 473–504.

(432) Mark 9, 38–40.

(433) *RCIA* 218–236, summarized.

(434) 32–71, summarized.

(435) *RC* 21–27, summarized.

(436) *Lutheran Book of Worship,* pp. 121–125, summarized.

(437) Ibid., pp. 198–201, summarized.

(438) *Lutheran Worship,* pp. 199–204, summarized.

(439) Ibid., pp. 205–207, summarized.

(440) *Holy Baptism and Services for the Renewal of Baptism,* pp. 22–39, summarized.

(441) Ibid., pp. 73–77, summarized.

(442) *The Book of Common Prayer,* pp. 299–311, summarized.

(443) Ibid., pp. 413–419, summarized.

(444) *The United Methodist Hymnal,* pp. 33–39, summarized.

(445) Ibid., pp. 45–49, summarized.

(446) *The Order of Baptism and Confirmation According to The Byzantine Rite of the Catholic Church,* summarized.

(447) Excerpts translated by author from AAS 2 (1910):577–583 *passim*. A full translation may be found in *Official Catholic Teachings: Worship & Liturgy*, ed. James J. Megivern (Wilmington: McGrath Publishing Company, 1978), pp. 33–41.

(448) AAS 23 (1931):353.

(449) *Canon Law Digest* 1:348–349. AAS 24 (1932):271.

(450) AAS 27 (1935):11–22, excerpt.

(451) III, q. 73, art. 8, ad 4.

(452) Benedict XIV, *De Synodo Dioecesana*, Lib. VII. Cap. X, nn. 5, 6, 7.

(453) *Canon Law Digest* 2:187; AAS 27:16.

(454) AAS 38 (1946):349–354.

(455) Ibid., p. 350.

(456) AAS 44 (1952):496–497.

(457) Ibid., p. 496.

Bibliographies

(Grouped according to the seven models explained in the text.)

1. ADULT INITIATION

Brown, Kathy and Sokol, Frank C. et al. *Issues in the Christian Initiation of Children: Catechesis and Liturgy.* Chicago: Liturgy Training Publications, 1989.

Code of Canon Law. Washington D.C.: Canon Law Society of America, 1983.

John Paul II. "On Evangelization in the Modern World." *Evangelii nuntiandi.* 8 December 1975.

Kavanagh, Aidan. *Confirmation: Origins and Reform.* New York: Pueblo, 1988.

————. "Response." *Worship* 65/4 (July, 1991):337–338.

The New Dictionary of Sacramental Worship. Ed. Peter E. Fink, S.J. Collegeville: The Liturgical Press, 1990.

Osborne, Kenan B., O.F.M. *The Christian Sacraments of Initiation: Baptism, Confirmation, Eucharist.* New York: Paulist Press, 1987.

Turner, Paul. "Confirmation: No More Winging It!" *Modern Liturgy* 18/7 (September, 1991):6–8.

———. *Sources of Confirmation from the Fathers Through the Reformers.* Collegeville: The Liturgical Press, 1993.

———. *The Meaning and Practice of Confirmation: Perspectives from a Sixteenth-Century Controversy.* Bern: Peter Lang, 1987.

———. "The Origins of Confirmation: An Analysis of Aidan Kavanagh's Hypothesis." *Worship* 65/4 (July, 1991):320–336.

Vatican Council II: The Conciliar and Postconciliar Documents. Ed. Austin Flannery, O.P. Collegeville: The Liturgical Press, 1975.

Whitaker, E. C. *Documents of the Baptismal Liturgy.* Slough: SPCK, 1970.

Yarnold, Edward, S.J. *The Awe-Inspiring Rites of Initiation: Baptismal Homilies of the Fourth Century.* Slough: St. Paul Publications, 1971.

2. CHRISMATION

Calivas, Alkiviadis. "The Sacramental Life in the Orthodox Church." *A Companion to the Greek Orthodox Church.* Ed. Fotios K. Litsas. New York: Greek Orthodox Archdiocese of North and South America, 1990.

Code of Canons of the Eastern Churches. Washington, D.C.: Canon Law Society of America, 1992.

Kucharek, Casimir. *The Sacramental Mysteries: A Byzantine Approach.* Allendale: Alleluia Press, 1976.

Ligier, Louis. *La Confirmation: Sens et conjoncture oecuménique hier et aujourd'hui.* Théologie Historique 23. Paris: Beauchesne, 1973.

Malouf, Lucien. *Byzantine Melkite Thinking.* Beirut: Technogravure et Presse Libanaises, 1972.

The Order of Baptism and Confirmation According to the Byzantine Rite of the Catholic Church. Pittsburgh: Byzantine Seminary Press, 1955.

Petras, David M. *Confirmation in the American Catholic Church: A Byzantine Perspective.* Washington: NCDD, 1980.

Pujol, Clemente, S.J. "Disciplina pastoralis in sacramentis codicis orientalis: Commentarium." *Notitiae* 292 (November, 1990):679–684.

3. PROTESTANT-ANGLICAN CHURCHES

The Book of Common Prayer and Administration of the Sacraments and Other Rites and Ceremonies of the Church, Together with The Psalter or Psalms of David, According to the Use of the Episcopal Church. New York: The Church Hymnal Corporation, 1979.

The Book of Discipline of the United Methodist Church, 1988. Nashville: The United Methodist Publishing House, 1988.

The Commission on Worship of The Lutheran Church—Missouri Synod. *Lutheran Worship.* St. Louis: Concordia Publishing House, 1982.

Constitutions & Canons for the Government of the Protestant Episcopal Church in the United States of America, Otherwise Known as The Episcopal Church, Adopted in General Conventions, 1789–1991, Together with the Rules of Order, Revised by the Convention 1991. (No publication data.)

Hickman, Hoyt L. *United Methodist Worship.* Nashville: Abingdon Press, 1991.

The Inter-Lutheran Commission on Worship. *Lutheran Book of Worship.* Minneapolis: Augsburg Publishing House, 1982.

Klos, Frank W. *Confirmation and First Communion: A Study Book.* Minneapolis: Augsburg Publishing House, 1968.

The Office of the General Assembly. *The Constitution of the Presbyterian Church (U.S.A.), Part II: Book of Order.* Louisville: The Office of the General Assembly, 1991.

The Office of Worship for the Presbyterian Church (U.S.A.) and the Cumberland Presbyterian Church. *Holy Baptism and Services for the Renewal of Baptism.* The Worship of God: Supplemental Liturgical Resource 2. Philadelphia: The Westminster Press, 1985.

Pfatteicher, Philip H. and Messerli, Carlos R. *Manual on the Liturgy, Lutheran Book of Worship.* Minneapolis: Augsburg Publishing House, 1979.

Stevick, Daniel B. *Baptismal Moments; Baptismal Meanings.* New York: The Church Hymnal Corporation, 1987.

The United Methodist Hymnal: Book of United Methodist Worship. Nashville: The United Methodist Publishing House, 1989.

4. CATHOLIC INITIATION

Englert, Clement C. *Catholics and Orthodox: Can They Unite?* New York: Paulist Press, 1961.

Meyendorff, John. *The Orthodox Church: Its Past and Its Role in the World Today.* New York: Pantheon Books, 1962.

Rite of Christian Initiation of Adults 473–504.

Vatican Council II. "Decree on Ecumenism." *Unitatis redintegratio.* 21 November 1964.

————. "On Admitting Other Christians to Eucharistic Communion in the Catholic Church." *In quibus rerum circumstantiis.* 1 June 1972.

Ware, Timothy. *The Orthodox Church.* Harmondsworth: Penguin Books, 1973.

5. CONFIRMATION OF CHILDREN

Almade, Frank D., et al. *When Should We Confirm? The Order of Initiation.* Ed. James A. Wilde. Chicago: Liturgy Training Publications, 1989.

Austin, Gerard. *Anointing with the Spirit—The Rite of Confirmation: The Use of Oil and Chrism.* New York: Pueblo Publishing Company, 1985.

Botte, Bernard. *From Silence to Participation: An Insider's View of Liturgical Renewal.* Trans. John Sullivan, O.C.D. Washington: The Pastoral Press, 1988.

Bugnini, Annibale. *The Reform of the Liturgy, 1948–1975.* Trans. Matthew J. O'Connell. Collegeville: The Liturgical Press, 1990.

The Code of Canon Law: A Text and Commentary. Ed. James A. Coriden, Thomas J. Green, and Donald E. Heintschel. New York: Paulist Press, 1985.

Doyle, Katherine, S.M. "Walking the Path to Restored Sequence: A Diocesan Experience." *Pace* 21 (1990–1991):88–91.

Duggan, Robert and Maureen Kelly. *Christian Initiation of Children: Hope for the Future.* New York: Paulist Press, 1991.

Huels, John M. O.S.M., J.C.D. *The Pastoral Companion: A Canon Law Handbook for Catholic Ministry.* Chicago: The Franciscan Herald Press, 1986.

McKenzie, Terri M. "Restoring the Sequence of the Sacraments of Initiation." *Pace* 21 (1990–1991):119–122.

Quinn, Frank C. et al. *Confirmed as Children, Affirmed as Teens: The Order of Initiation.* Ed. James A. Wilde. Chicago: Liturgy Training Publications, 1990.

Rite of Baptism for Children. The Rites. Trans. International Commission on English in the Liturgy. New York: Pueblo Publishing Co., 1976.

Rite of Blessing of Oils. Rite of Consecrating the Chrism. The Rites.

Rite of Confirmation. The Rites.

Searle, Mark. *The Church Speaks about Sacraments with Children: Baptism, Confirmation, Eucharist, Penance.* Chicago: Liturgy Training Publications, 1990.

Sharing the Light of Faith: National Catechetical Directory for Catholics of the United States. Washington: U. S. Catholic Conference, 1979.

Vatican II. "Constitution on the Sacred Liturgy." *Sacrosanctum concilium.* 4 December 1963.

———. "Dogmatic Constitution on the Church." *Lumen gentium.* 21 November 1964.

Winkler, Gabriele. "Confirmation or Chrismation? A Study in Comparative Liturgy." *Worship* 58/1 (January, 1984):2–17.

6. ADOLESCENT CONFIRMATION

Bausch, William J. *A New Look at the Sacraments.* Revised Edition. Mystic: Twenty-Third Publications, 1986.

Doyle, Eric, O.F.M., "Confirmation for Commitment to Mission." *The Clergy Review* 67/5 (May, 1982):162–165.

Huels, John M. "The Age of Confirmation: A Canonist's View." *Catechumenate* 9 (November, 1987):30–36.

Kubick, Art. "More About Confirmation: Some Recent Approaches." *Pace* 17 (1986–87):183–186; 205–208; 239–243.

———. "Confirmation Notes 1986–87." Pace 18 (1987–88):227–230; 254–257.

———. "Confirmation Notes: Current Developments." *Pace* 19 (1988–89):34–37; 66–70; 93–97.

———. "Confirmation Notes: 1989–91." *Pace* 21 (1991):11–15; 48–52.

Marsh, Thomas A. et al. *Confirming the Faith of Adolescents.* Arthur J. Kubick, ed. New York: Paulist Press, 1991.

Marsh, Thomas A. *Gift of Community: Baptism and Confirmation.* Message of the Sacraments, vol. 2. Ed. Monika K. Hellwig. Wilmington: Michael Glazier, Inc., 1984.

Martos, Joseph. "Confirmation at the Crossroads." *The Living Light* 28/3 (Spring, 1992):225–239.

———. "Confirmation: The Debate Continues." *Gifts* 1 (1991):5–7.

———. *Doors to the Sacred: A Historical Introduction to the Sacraments in the Catholic Church.* Expanded Edition. Tarrytown: Triumph Books, 1991.

McKenzie, Terri and Savelesky, Michael J. "Confirmation with First Communion? It Works!" *Chicago Catechumenate* (May 1986):16–23.

Roberto, John. "Confirmation in the American Catholic Church." *The Living Light* 15/2 (Summer, 1978):262–279. Or Washington:NCDD, 1978.

Sacred Congregation of the Discipline of the Sacraments. "Decree, *Quam singulari.*" Megivern, James J. *Worship & Liturgy.* A Consortium Book. Wilmington: McGrath Publishing Company, 1978.

Sacred Congregation for the Doctrine of the Faith. "Instruction on Infant Baptism." *Pastoralis actio.* 20 October 1980.

Sawyer, Kieran. "Confirmation Dilemma: A Conflict of Principles." *Gifts* (Winter, 1990):2–3.

———. *Confirming Faith.* Notre Dame: Ave Maria Press, 1982.

Searle, Mark. "Confirmation: The State of the Question." *Church* (Winter, 1985):15–23.

Segundo, Juan Luis, S.J., and the Staff of the Peter Faber Center in Montevideo, Uruguay. *The Sacraments Today.* Trans. John Drury. A Theology for Artisans of a New Humanity, vol. 4. New York: Maryknoll, 1974.

Weakland, Rembert. Foreword to *Confirming Faith* by Kieran Sawyer. Notre Dame: Ave Maria Press, 1982.

Zanzig, Thomas. *Celebrating Confirmation.* Winona: Saint Mary's Press, 1990.

7. CONFIRMATION IN DANGER OF DEATH

Order of Christian Funerals. Chicago: Liturgy Training Publications, 1989.

Rite of Anointing and Pastoral Care of the Sick. The Rites. New York: Pueblo Publishing Co., 1976.

Index